Mometrix
TEST PREPARATION

Series 30
Exam Secrets
Study Guide

DEAR FUTURE EXAM SUCCESS STORY

First of all, **THANK YOU** for purchasing Mometrix study materials!

Second, congratulations! You are one of the few determined test-takers who are committed to doing whatever it takes to excel on your exam. **You have come to the right place.** We developed these study materials with one goal in mind: to deliver you the information you need in a format that's concise and easy to use.

In addition to optimizing your guide for the content of the test, we've outlined our recommended steps for breaking down the preparation process into small, attainable goals so you can make sure you stay on track.

We've also analyzed the entire test-taking process, identifying the most common pitfalls and showing how you can overcome them and be ready for any curveball the test throws you.

Standardized testing is one of the biggest obstacles on your road to success, which only increases the importance of doing well in the high-pressure, high-stakes environment of test day. Your results on this test could have a significant impact on your future, and this guide provides the information and practical advice to help you achieve your full potential on test day.

Your success is our success

We would love to hear from you! If you would like to share the story of your exam success or if you have any questions or comments in regard to our products, please contact us at **800-673-8175** or **support@mometrix.com**.

Thanks again for your business and we wish you continued success!

Sincerely,
The Mometrix Test Preparation Team

> **Need more help? Check out our flashcards at:**
> **http://MometrixFlashcards.com/Series30**

TABLE OF CONTENTS

Introduction

Thank you for purchasing this resource! You have made the choice to prepare yourself for a test that could have a huge impact on your future, and this guide is designed to help you be fully ready for test day. Obviously, it's important to have a solid understanding of the test material, but you also need to be prepared for the unique environment and stressors of the test, so that you can perform to the best of your abilities.

For this purpose, the first section that appears in this guide is the **Secret Keys**. We've devoted countless hours to meticulously researching what works and what doesn't, and we've boiled down our findings to the five most impactful steps you can take to improve your performance on the test. We start at the beginning with study planning and move through the preparation process, all the way to the testing strategies that will help you get the most out of what you know when you're finally sitting in front of the test.

We recommend that you start preparing for your test as far in advance as possible. However, if you've bought this guide as a last-minute study resource and only have a few days before your test, we recommend that you skip over the first two Secret Keys since they address a long-term study plan.

If you struggle with **test anxiety**, we strongly encourage you to check out our recommendations for how you can overcome it. Test anxiety is a formidable foe, but it can be beaten, and we want to make sure you have the tools you need to defeat it.

1

Secret Key 1: Plan Big, Study Small

There's a lot riding on your performance. If you want to ace this test, you're going to need to keep your skills sharp and the material fresh in your mind. You need a plan that lets you review everything you need to know while still fitting in your schedule. We'll break this strategy down into three categories.

Information Organization

Start with the information you already have: the official test outline. From this, you can make a complete list of all the concepts you need to cover before the test. Organize these concepts into groups that can be studied together, and create a list of any related vocabulary you need to learn so you can brush up on any difficult terms. You'll want to keep this vocabulary list handy once you actually start studying since you may need to add to it along the way.

Time Management

Once you have your set of study concepts, decide how to spread them out over the time you have left before the test. Break your study plan into small, clear goals so you have a manageable task for each day and know exactly what you're doing. Then just focus on one small step at a time. When you manage your time this way, you don't need to spend hours at a time studying. Studying a small block of content for a short period each day helps you retain information better and avoid stressing over how much you have left to do. You can relax knowing that you have a plan to cover everything in time. In order for this strategy to be effective though, you have to start studying early and stick to your schedule. Avoid the exhaustion and futility that comes from last-minute cramming!

Study Environment

The environment you study in has a big impact on your learning. Studying in a coffee shop, while probably more enjoyable, is not likely to be as fruitful as studying in a quiet room. It's important to keep distractions to a minimum. You're only planning to study for a short block of time, so make the most of it. Don't pause to check your phone or get up to find a snack. It's also important to **avoid multitasking**. Research has consistently shown that multitasking will make your studying dramatically less effective. Your study area should also be comfortable and well-lit so you don't have the distraction of straining your eyes or sitting on an uncomfortable chair.

 The time of day you study is also important. You want to be rested and alert. Don't wait until just before bedtime. Study when you'll be most likely to comprehend and remember. Even better, if you know what time of day your test will be, set that time aside for study. That way your brain will be used to working on that subject at that specific time and you'll have a better chance of recalling information.

Finally, it can be helpful to team up with others who are studying for the same test. Your actual studying should be done in as isolated an environment as possible, but the work of organizing the information and setting up the study plan can be divided up. In between study sessions, you can discuss with your teammates the concepts that you're all studying and quiz each other on the details. Just be sure that your teammates are as serious about the test as you are. If you find that your study time is being replaced with social time, you might need to find a new team.

Secret Key 2: Make Your Studying Count

You're devoting a lot of time and effort to preparing for this test, so you want to be absolutely certain it will pay off. This means doing more than just reading the content and hoping you can remember it on test day. It's important to make every minute of study count. There are two main areas you can focus on to make your studying count.

Retention

It doesn't matter how much time you study if you can't remember the material. You need to make sure you are retaining the concepts. To check your retention of the information you're learning, try recalling it at later times with minimal prompting. Try carrying around flashcards and glance at one or two from time to time or ask a friend who's also studying for the test to quiz you.

To enhance your retention, look for ways to put the information into practice so that you can apply it rather than simply recalling it. If you're using the information in practical ways, it will be much easier to remember. Similarly, it helps to solidify a concept in your mind if you're not only reading it to yourself but also explaining it to someone else. Ask a friend to let you teach them about a concept you're a little shaky on (or speak aloud to an imaginary audience if necessary). As you try to summarize, define, give examples, and answer your friend's questions, you'll understand the concepts better and they will stay with you longer. Finally, step back for a big picture view and ask yourself how each piece of information fits with the whole subject. When you link the different concepts together and see them working together as a whole, it's easier to remember the individual components.

Finally, practice showing your work on any multi-step problems, even if you're just studying. Writing out each step you take to solve a problem will help solidify the process in your mind, and you'll be more likely to remember it during the test.

Modality

Modality simply refers to the means or method by which you study. Choosing a study modality that fits your own individual learning style is crucial. No two people learn best in exactly the same way, so it's important to know your strengths and use them to your advantage.

4

For example, if you learn best by visualization, focus on visualizing a concept in your mind and draw an image or a diagram. Try color-coding your notes, illustrating them, or creating symbols that will trigger your mind to recall a learned concept. If you learn best by hearing or discussing information, find a study partner who learns the same way or read aloud to yourself. Think about how to put the information in your own words. Imagine that you are giving a lecture on the topic and record yourself so you can listen to it later.

For any learning style, flashcards can be helpful. Organize the information so you can take advantage of spare moments to review. Underline key words or phrases. Use different colors for different categories. Mnemonic devices (such as creating a short list in which every item starts with the same letter) can also help with retention. Find what works best for you and use it to store the information in your mind most effectively and easily.

Secret Key 3: Practice the Right Way

Your success on test day depends not only on how many hours you put into preparing, but also on whether you prepared the right way. It's good to check along the way to see if your studying is paying off. One of the most effective ways to do this is by taking practice tests to evaluate your progress. Practice tests are useful because they show exactly where you need to improve. Every time you take a practice test, pay special attention to these three groups of questions:

- The questions you got wrong
- The questions you had to guess on, even if you guessed right
- The questions you found difficult or slow to work through

This will show you exactly what your weak areas are, and where you need to devote more study time. Ask yourself why each of these questions gave you trouble. Was it because you didn't understand the material? Was it because you didn't remember the vocabulary? Do you need more repetitions on this type of question to build speed and confidence? Dig into those questions and figure out how you can strengthen your weak areas as you go back to review the material.

 Additionally, many practice tests have a section explaining the answer choices. It can be tempting to read the explanation and think that you now have a good understanding of the concept. However, an explanation likely only covers part of the question's broader context. Even if the explanation makes perfect sense, **go back and investigate** every concept related to the question until you're positive you have a thorough understanding.

As you go along, keep in mind that the practice test is just that: practice. Memorizing these questions and answers will not be very helpful on the actual test because it is unlikely to have any of the same exact questions. If you only know the right answers to the sample questions, you won't be prepared for the real thing. **Study the concepts** until you understand them fully, and then you'll be able to answer any question that shows up on the test.

It's important to wait on the practice tests until you're ready. If you take a test on your first day of study, you may be overwhelmed by the amount of material covered and how much you need to learn. Work up to it gradually.

On test day, you'll need to be prepared for answering questions, managing your time, and using the test-taking strategies you've learned. It's a lot to balance, like a mental marathon that will have a big impact on your future. Like training for a marathon, you'll need to start slowly and work your way up. When test day arrives, you'll be ready.

Start with the strategies you've read in the first two Secret Keys—plan your course and study in the way that works best for you. If you have time, consider using multiple study resources to get different approaches to the same concepts. It can be helpful to see difficult concepts from more than one angle. Then find a good source for practice tests. Many times, the test website will suggest potential study resources or provide sample tests.

Practice Test Strategy

If you're able to find at least three practice tests, we recommend this strategy:

UNTIMED AND OPEN-BOOK PRACTICE

Take the first test with no time constraints and with your notes and study guide handy. Take your time and focus on applying the strategies you've learned.

TIMED AND OPEN-BOOK PRACTICE

Take the second practice test open-book as well, but set a timer and practice pacing yourself to finish in time.

TIMED AND CLOSED-BOOK PRACTICE

Take any other practice tests as if it were test day. Set a timer and put away your study materials. Sit at a table or desk in a quiet room, imagine yourself at the testing center, and answer questions as quickly and accurately as possible.

Keep repeating timed and closed-book tests on a regular basis until you run out of practice tests or it's time for the actual test. Your mind will be ready for the schedule and stress of test day, and you'll be able to focus on recalling the material you've learned.

Secret Key 4: Pace Yourself

Once you're fully prepared for the material on the test, your biggest challenge on test day will be managing your time. Just knowing that the clock is ticking can make you panic even if you have plenty of time left. Work on pacing yourself so you can build confidence against the time constraints of the exam. Pacing is a difficult skill to master, especially in a high-pressure environment, so **practice is vital**.

Set time expectations for your pace based on how much time is available. For example, if a section has 60 questions and the time limit is 30 minutes, you know you have to average 30 seconds or less per question in order to answer them all. Although 30 seconds is the hard limit, set 25 seconds per question as your goal, so you reserve extra time to spend on harder questions. When you budget extra time for the harder questions, you no longer have any reason to stress when those questions take longer to answer.

Don't let this time expectation distract you from working through the test at a calm, steady pace, but keep it in mind so you don't spend too much time on any one question. Recognize that taking extra time on one question you don't understand may keep you from answering two that you do understand later in the test. If your time limit for a question is up and you're still not sure of the answer, mark it and move on, and come back to it later if the time and the test format allow. If the testing format doesn't allow you to return to earlier questions, just make an educated guess; then put it out of your mind and move on.

On the easier questions, be careful not to rush. It may seem wise to hurry through them so you have more time for the challenging ones, but it's not worth missing one if you know the concept and just didn't take the time to read the question fully. Work efficiently but make sure you understand the question and have looked at all of the answer choices, since more than one may seem right at first.

Even if you're paying attention to the time, you may find yourself a little behind at some point. You should speed up to get back on track, but do so wisely. Don't panic; just take a few seconds less on each question until you're caught up. Don't guess without thinking, but do look through the answer choices and eliminate any you know are wrong. If you can get down to two choices, it is often worthwhile to guess from those. Once you've chosen an answer, move on and don't dwell on any that you skipped or had to hurry through. If a question was taking too long, chances are it was one of the harder ones, so you weren't as likely to get it right anyway.

On the other hand, if you find yourself getting ahead of schedule, it may be beneficial to slow down a little. The more quickly you work, the more likely you are to make a careless mistake that will affect your score. You've budgeted time for each question, so don't be afraid to spend that time. Practice an efficient but careful pace to get the most out of the time you have.

Secret Key 5: Have a Plan for Guessing

When you're taking the test, you may find yourself stuck on a question. Some of the answer choices seem better than others, but you don't see the one answer choice that is obviously correct. What do you do?

The scenario described above is very common, yet most test takers have not effectively prepared for it. Developing and practicing a plan for guessing may be one of the single most effective uses of your time as you get ready for the exam.

In developing your plan for guessing, there are three questions to address:

- When should you start the guessing process?
- How should you narrow down the choices?
- Which answer should you choose?

When to Start the Guessing Process

Unless your plan for guessing is to select C every time (which, despite its merits, is not what we recommend), you need to leave yourself enough time to apply your answer elimination strategies. Since you have a limited amount of time for each question, that means that if you're going to give yourself the best shot at guessing correctly, you have to decide quickly whether or not you will guess.

Of course, the best-case scenario is that you don't have to guess at all, so first, see if you can answer the question based on your knowledge of the subject and basic reasoning skills. Focus on the key words in the question and try to jog your memory of related topics. Give yourself a chance to bring the knowledge to mind, but once you realize that you don't have (or you can't access) the knowledge you need to answer the question, it's time to start the guessing process.

It's almost always better to start the guessing process too early than too late. It only takes a few seconds to remember something and answer the question from knowledge. Carefully eliminating wrong answer choices takes longer. Plus, going through the process of eliminating answer choices can actually help jog your memory.

Summary: Start the guessing process as soon as you decide that you can't answer the question based on your knowledge.

10

How to Narrow Down the Choices

The next chapter in this book (**Test-Taking Strategies**) includes a wide range of strategies for how to approach questions and how to look for answer choices to eliminate. You will definitely want to read those carefully, practice them, and figure out which ones work best for you. Here though, we're going to address a mindset rather than a particular strategy.

Your odds of guessing an answer correctly depend on how many options you are choosing from.

Number of options left	5	4	3	2	1
Odds of guessing correctly	20%	25%	33%	50%	100%

You can see from this chart just how valuable it is to be able to eliminate incorrect answers and make an educated guess, but there are two things that many test takers do that cause them to miss out on the benefits of guessing:

- Accidentally eliminating the correct answer
- Selecting an answer based on an impression

We'll look at the first one here, and the second one in the next section.

To avoid accidentally eliminating the correct answer, we recommend a thought exercise called **the $5 challenge**. In this challenge, you only eliminate an answer choice from contention if you are willing to bet $5 on it being wrong. Why $5? Five dollars is a small but not insignificant amount of money. It's an amount you could

afford to lose but wouldn't want to throw away. And while losing $5 once might not hurt too much, doing it twenty times will set you back $100. In the same way, each small decision you make—eliminating a choice here, guessing on a question there—won't by itself impact your score very much, but when you put them all together, they can make a big difference. By holding each answer choice elimination decision to a higher standard, you can reduce the risk of accidentally eliminating the correct answer.

The $5 challenge can also be applied in a positive sense: If you are willing to bet $5 that an answer choice *is* correct, go ahead and mark it as correct.

Summary: Only eliminate an answer choice if you are willing to bet $5 that it is wrong.

Which Answer to Choose

You're taking the test. You've run into a hard question and decided you'll have to guess. You've eliminated all the answer choices you're willing to bet $5 on. Now you have to pick an answer. Why do we even need to talk about this? Why can't you just pick whichever one you feel like when the time comes?

The answer to these questions is that if you don't come into the test with a plan, you'll rely on your impression to select an answer choice, and if you do that, you risk falling into a trap. The test writers know that everyone who takes their test will be guessing on some of the questions, so they intentionally write wrong answer choices to seem plausible. You still have to pick an answer though, and if the wrong answer choices are designed to look right, how can you ever be sure that you're not falling for their trap? The best solution we've found to this dilemma is to take the decision out of your hands entirely. Here is the process we recommend:

Once you've eliminated any choices that you are confident (willing to bet $5) are wrong, select the first remaining choice as your answer.

Whether you choose to select the first remaining choice, the second, or the last, the important thing is that you use some preselected standard. Using this approach guarantees that you will not be enticed into selecting an answer choice that looks right, because you are not basing your decision on how the answer choices look.

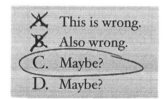

This is not meant to make you question your knowledge. Instead, it is to help you recognize the difference between your knowledge and your impressions. There's a huge difference between thinking an answer is right because of what you know, and thinking an answer is right because it looks or sounds like it should be right.

Summary: To ensure that your selection is appropriately random, make a predetermined selection from among all answer choices you have not eliminated.

Test-Taking Strategies

This section contains a list of test-taking strategies that you may find helpful as you work through the test. By taking what you know and applying logical thought, you can maximize your chances of answering any question correctly!

It is very important to realize that every question is different and every person is different: no single strategy will work on every question, and no single strategy will work for every person. That's why we've included all of them here, so you can try them out and determine which ones work best for different types of questions and which ones work best for you.

Question Strategies

⊘ READ CAREFULLY

Read the question and the answer choices carefully. Don't miss the question because you misread the terms. You have plenty of time to read each question thoroughly and make sure you understand what is being asked. Yet a happy medium must be attained, so don't waste too much time. You must read carefully and efficiently.

⊘ CONTEXTUAL CLUES

Look for contextual clues. If the question includes a word you are not familiar with, look at the immediate context for some indication of what the word might mean. Contextual clues can often give you all the information you need to decipher the meaning of an unfamiliar word. Even if you can't determine the meaning, you may be able to narrow down the possibilities enough to make a solid guess at the answer to the question.

⊘ PREFIXES

If you're having trouble with a word in the question or answer choices, try dissecting it. Take advantage of every clue that the word might include. Prefixes and suffixes can be a huge help. Usually, they allow you to determine a basic meaning. *Pre-* means before, *post-* means after, *pro-* is positive, *de-* is negative. From prefixes and suffixes, you can get an idea of the general meaning of the word and try to put it into context.

⊘ HEDGE WORDS

Watch out for critical hedge words, such as *likely, may, can, sometimes, often, almost, mostly, usually, generally, rarely,* and *sometimes.* Question writers insert these hedge phrases to cover every possibility. Often an answer choice will be wrong simply because it leaves no room for exception. Be on guard for answer choices that have definitive words such as *exactly* and *always.*

⊘ Switchback Words

Stay alert for *switchbacks*. These are the words and phrases frequently used to alert you to shifts in thought. The most common switchback words are *but*, *although*, and *however*. Others include *nevertheless*, *on the other hand*, *even though*, *while*, *in spite of*, *despite*, and *regardless of*. Switchback words are important to catch because they can change the direction of the question or an answer choice.

⊘ Face Value

When in doubt, use common sense. Accept the situation in the problem at face value. Don't read too much into it. These problems will not require you to make wild assumptions. If you have to go beyond creativity and warp time or space in order to have an answer choice fit the question, then you should move on and consider the other answer choices. These are normal problems rooted in reality. The applicable relationship or explanation may not be readily apparent, but it is there for you to figure out. Use your common sense to interpret anything that isn't clear.

Answer Choice Strategies

⊘ Answer Selection

The most thorough way to pick an answer choice is to identify and eliminate wrong answers until only one is left, then confirm it is the correct answer. Sometimes an answer choice may immediately seem right, but be careful. The test writers will usually put more than one reasonable answer choice on each question, so take a second to read all of them and make sure that the other choices are not equally obvious. As long as you have time left, it is better to read every answer choice than to pick the first one that looks right without checking the others.

⊘ Answer Choice Families

An answer choice family consists of two (in rare cases, three) answer choices that are very similar in construction and cannot all be true at the same time. If you see two answer choices that are direct opposites or parallels, one of them is usually the correct answer. For instance, if one answer choice says that quantity x increases and another either says that quantity x decreases (opposite) or says that quantity y increases (parallel), then those answer choices would fall into the same family. An answer choice that doesn't match the construction of the answer choice family is more likely to be incorrect. Most questions will not have answer choice families, but when they do appear, you should be prepared to recognize them.

⊘ Eliminate Answers

Eliminate answer choices as soon as you realize they are wrong, but make sure you consider all possibilities. If you are eliminating answer choices and realize that the last one you are left with is also wrong, don't panic. Start over and consider each choice again. There may be something you missed the first time that you will realize on the second pass.

⊘ Avoid Fact Traps

Don't be distracted by an answer choice that is factually true but doesn't answer the question. You are looking for the choice that answers the question. Stay focused on what the question is asking for so you don't accidentally pick an answer that is true but incorrect. Always go back to the question and make sure the answer choice you've selected actually answers the question and is not merely a true statement.

⊘ Extreme Statements

In general, you should avoid answers that put forth extreme actions as standard practice or proclaim controversial ideas as established fact. An answer choice that states the "process should be used in certain situations, if..." is much more likely to be correct than one that states the "process should be discontinued completely." The first is a calm rational statement and doesn't even make a definitive, uncompromising stance, using a hedge word *if* to provide wiggle room, whereas the second choice is far more extreme.

⊘ Benchmark

As you read through the answer choices and you come across one that seems to answer the question well, mentally select that answer choice. This is not your final answer, but it's the one that will help you evaluate the other answer choices. The one that you selected is your benchmark or standard for judging each of the other answer choices. Every other answer choice must be compared to your benchmark. That choice is correct until proven otherwise by another answer choice beating it. If you find a better answer, then that one becomes your new benchmark. Once you've decided that no other choice answers the question as well as your benchmark, you have your final answer.

⊘ Predict the Answer

Before you even start looking at the answer choices, it is often best to try to predict the answer. When you come up with the answer on your own, it is easier to avoid distractions and traps because you will know exactly what to look for. The right answer choice is unlikely to be word-for-word what you came up with, but it should be a close match. Even if you are confident that you have the right answer, you should still take the time to read each option before moving on.

General Strategies

⊘ Tough Questions

If you are stumped on a problem or it appears too hard or too difficult, don't waste time. Move on! Remember though, if you can quickly check for obviously incorrect answer choices, your chances of guessing correctly are greatly improved. Before you completely give up, at least try to knock out a couple of possible answers. Eliminate what you can and then guess at the remaining answer choices before moving on.

⊘ CHECK YOUR WORK

Since you will probably not know every term listed and the answer to every question, it is important that you get credit for the ones that you do know. Don't miss any questions through careless mistakes. If at all possible, try to take a second to look back over your answer selection and make sure you've selected the correct answer choice and haven't made a costly careless mistake (such as marking an answer choice that you didn't mean to mark). This quick double check should more than pay for itself in caught mistakes for the time it costs.

⊘ PACE YOURSELF

It's easy to be overwhelmed when you're looking at a page full of questions; your mind is confused and full of random thoughts, and the clock is ticking down faster than you would like. Calm down and maintain the pace that you have set for yourself. Especially as you get down to the last few minutes of the test, don't let the small numbers on the clock make you panic. As long as you are on track by monitoring your pace, you are guaranteed to have time for each question.

⊘ DON'T RUSH

It is very easy to make errors when you are in a hurry. Maintaining a fast pace in answering questions is pointless if it makes you miss questions that you would have gotten right otherwise. Test writers like to include distracting information and wrong answers that seem right. Taking a little extra time to avoid careless mistakes can make all the difference in your test score. Find a pace that allows you to be confident in the answers that you select.

⊘ KEEP MOVING

Panicking will not help you pass the test, so do your best to stay calm and keep moving. Taking deep breaths and going through the answer elimination steps you practiced can help to break through a stress barrier and keep your pace.

Final Notes

The combination of a solid foundation of content knowledge and the confidence that comes from practicing your plan for applying that knowledge is the key to maximizing your performance on test day. As your foundation of content knowledge is built up and strengthened, you'll find that the strategies included in this chapter become more and more effective in helping you quickly sift through the distractions and traps of the test to isolate the correct answer.

Now that you're preparing to move forward into the test content chapters of this book, be sure to keep your goal in mind. As you read, think about how you will be able to apply this information on the test. If you've already seen sample questions for the test and you have an idea of the question format and style, try to come up with questions of your own that you can answer based on what you're reading. This will give you valuable practice applying your knowledge in the same ways you can expect to on test day.

Good luck and good studying!

18

General

NFA

ROLE IN SUPPORTING THE CFTC

The Commodities Exchange Act (CEA) of 1936 was created to regulate the actions of commodities traders engaged in trading futures contracts, options on futures contracts, options on physical commodities, security futures products, and some retail foreign exchange contracts. The act is administered by the Commodity Futures Trading Commission (CFTC). Section 17 of the CEA provides for the registration of industry self-regulating organizations with the CFTC, which play in role in regulating the actions of their members. The National Futures Association (NFA) is the only such organization currently registered, and acts on behalf of the CFTC. The NFA is responsible for the following regulatory functions:

- auditing and surveillance of NFA members for the purpose of enforcing and ensuring compliance with NFA financial requirements
- establishment and enforcement of rules and standards to ensure customer protection
- administration and maintenance of an arbitration process to adjudicate disputes arising from futures and foreign exchange transactions
- determination of fitness of applicants for membership and review of continuing membership for existing members

MEMBERSHIP REQUIREMENTS

In 1978, legislation that amended the Commodity Exchange Act (CEA) was passed. It provided for mandatory membership in at least one futures association that would act in a regulatory capacity on behalf of the Commodity Futures Trading Commission (CFTC). Since the National Futures Association (NFA) is the only such registered futures association, the legislation effectively made NFA membership mandatory. The legislation, CFTC Regulation 170.15, applied only to futures commission merchants (FCMs). Article VI of the NFA Articles of Incorporation expanded the membership requirement to include the following futures professionals:

- commodity pool operator (CPO)
- commodity trading advisor (CTA)
- introducing broker (IB)
- leverage transaction merchant (LTM)

NFA by-law 1101 expressly prohibits any NFA member from accepting futures orders from any individuals or firms (except direct customers) that are not also members of the NFA.

NFA MEMBER AND NFA REGISTRANT

Any person registered with the Commodity Futures Trading Commission (CFTC) to conduct futures trading is eligible for membership in the NFA. In addition, any contract market (such as the CBOT, the CME, etc.) and any individual specifically qualified by a CFTC rule is eligible for membership. In addition, the following professionals are required by statute to become members of the NFA:

- futures transaction merchant (FCM)
- commodity pool operator (CPO)
- commodity trading advisor (CTA)
- introducing broker (IB)
- leverage transaction merchant (LTM)

In addition to the professions listed above, registration (but not membership) is required for the following professionals:

- floor broker (FB)
- floor trader (FT)
- associated person (AP)

Note that FBs and FTs are regulated by the exchange with which trading privileges are maintained.

TEMPORARY LICENSE

A Temporary License (TL) grants the recipient the right to act in the capacity of a either an AP (Associated Person) or an IB (Introducing Broker) subject to all CFTC rules, regulations, orders and all NFA requirements. The NFA can grant a Temporary License to any applicant for registration as an AP or IB, whose registration has not previously been suspended or revoked, upon properly filing the required completed forms with the NFA. A Form 8-R must be completed in the case of an AP. A Form 7-R must be completed in the case of IB. An IB also requires a qualified FCM to act as a sponsor. A Temporary License is not considered to be a registration. It is considered to be an associate membership in the NFA. In the case of an Associated Person, it is considered membership only if the applicant's sponsor is an NFA member.

BRANCH OFFICE

A branch office is any non -main site location where an FCM, IB, CPO, or CTA has employees engaged in activities that require registration with the NFA. Each branch office must have a branch manager, even if the manager is the only employee at the location. A manager can be manager of only one location. To have the status of branch manager, the employee must either apply for registration as an AP, or currently be registered as an AP. Managers should list their status as branch manager on their Form 8-R. A firm's NFA registration Form 7-R must include the names of all branch managers, and all branch office addresses. P.O. boxes are insufficient. New opening and closing of branch offices must also be promptly reported to NFA on form 7-R.

NFA BYLAW 1101

The NFA's Bylaw 1101 and CFTC Rule 170.15 state that any FCM, IB, CTA and CPO that transacts futures business with the public must become a member in the NFA. It prohibits an NFA Member from trading futures with non-Members or suspended Members.

There are some exceptions to the rule. A Member can accept futures orders from direct individual customers even if the person is not an NFA Member. Also, floor brokers and floor traders are regulated by the exchange, not the NFA, and so do not need to be Members of the NFA in order to trade with an NFA Member. Finally, if a person is registered, under section 17 of the Commodities Exchange Act, with another registered futures association, then they do not need to be an NFA Member in order to trade with NFA Members. However, the CPO, CTA, IB, or FCM that originates the orders, and everyone that is used to execute the orders in between, must be eligible to trade. The NFA Board has authority to exempt persons from this regulation.

NFA COMPLIANCE RULE 2-9

Each NFA Member firm must designate a person or persons to supervise its employees and agents in their commodity futures trading activities. The employee may also require supervision of their telemarketing activities if their employment history warrants it.

A Member firm should not permit an Associate employee to have discretionary control over a customer's commodity futures account, unless the Associate has had a minimum of two years of experience and has been registered continuously under the Act during that time. If an Associate can demonstrate that he/she has equivalent experience, then a waiver can be obtained for this requirement. To obtain a waiver, the Member must submit a written request to the Compliance Director and the request must be approved by a 3 person committee. This requirement does not apply to firms that are CTAs. Each Associate employee should be familiar with the firm's anti-money laundering program. Each Associate employee should have ongoing training as appropriate.

NFA'S DISCIPLINARY PROCESS

If a Member violates an NFA rule, then a report is prepared for and submitted to the Business Conduct Committee. If the committee finds the report to be valid, the committee then serves a formal complaint about the Member. The Member can appeal the complaint to the Appeals Committee. If the appeal is lost, then the NFA has the authority to discipline its Members in the form of penalties. The penalties that can be imposed on the Member include expulsion, suspension, censure, restrictions on associating with the violating Member, reprimand, or a fine not to exceed $250,000 per violation. If necessary, further action by the President may be taken to protect the markets, customers, or other Members from the violating Member.

NFA COMPLIANCE RULE 3-2

National Futures Association (NFA) Compliance Rule 2-9 requires that all members exercise an appropriate level of supervision over employees and agents. Necessary complaints must be submitted to the compliance director of the NFA Business Conduct Committee (BCC). According to Compliance Rule 3-2, the compliance director is required to issue a written report to the BCC that includes the following information:

- the reason for the initiation of the investigation
- a summary of the complaint, if a complaint was created
- the relevant facts of the investigation
- a recommendation for the BCC to proceed further (if applicable)

Once the compliance director issues a completed report to the Business Compliance Committee (BCC) of the National Futures Association (NFA) no later than four months from the date of the inception of the investigation, actions must be taken by the BCC. Within 30 days of receiving the report from the compliance director, the BCC must decide between two courses of action:

- If there is no reasonable basis to assume a violation has occurred, the BCC must close the matter.
- If there is reason to believe that a violation has occurred, the BCC must issue a formal written and dated complaint.

Upon completion of an investigation by the compliance director, the BCC of the National Futures Association (NFA) may, at the recommendation of the compliance director, issue a warning letter if there is no reason to believe that a violation has occurred.

If, as the result of an investigation, the Business Conduct Committee (BCC) of the National Futures Association (NFA) finds that a rule has been violated and a written and dated complaint is warranted, a complaint issued by the BCC must include the following information:

- each NFA violation alleged to have occurred, or each NFA violation that, but for the complaint, would have occurred
- each act or omission which precipitated the violation

WRITTEN NOTICE OF APPEAL

If the National Futures Association (NFA) arbitration hearing panel issues a decision against a respondent, the respondent has an opportunity to appeal. A respondent may file a written notice of appeal with the National Futures Association (NFA) within 15 days of the date on which the hearing panel issued its decision. The respondent must describe the elements of the decision that are the subject of the appeal, and must outline any request to personally appear before the panel.

ACTIONS TAKEN AGAINST NFA MEMBER PRIOR TO HEARING

With the agreement of the NFA's Board of Directors or the Executive Committee of the NFA, the president of the NFA may suspend the membership of the member or associate, restrict the operations of the member or associate (including his or her ability to associate with other members), or demand immediate remedial action by the member prior to a hearing.

PENALTIES

The penalties that may be imposed upon a violating member include:

- expulsion from the NFA or suspension for a specified time period
- suspension from association with another NFA member
- censure or reprimand
- a fine not exceeding $250,000 per violation
- an order to cease and desist
- any other penalty not inconsistent with this rule

SUPERVISOR'S ATTESTATION

The written Attestation of the supervisor states that the NFA's Self-Examination Checklist was used and whether the member firm did or did not sufficiently meet the supervision requirements as indicated by the Checklist. It should include the Member's name and branch location if applicable. It must be signed, dated, and kept on file for 5 years. The attestations **should not** be forwarded to the NFA, but should be readily available upon request. One signed and dated attestation letter is required for each office. Branch offices must send a copy of their signed and dated letter to the main office. Guaranteed IBs must submit their signed attestation letters to their guarantor FCM. Questions about the Checklist should be directed to the Compliance Department at 1-800-621-3570.

NFA'S SELF-EXAMINATION CHECKLIST

To comply with NFA rule 2-9, the NFA requires all member firms to submit to a self-administered annual checkup using the NFA's "Self-Examination Checklist". The Checklist is divided into 5 sections. The first section is the General checklist for all registrants. The remaining 4 sections are for FCM, IB, CPO, and CTA. These checklists must be used, when applicable, in addition to the general checklist. The checklist is updated as needed by the NFA. The most recent version of the checklist should be obtained when using it for the review, (www.nfa.futures.org). The checklist is meant to assess a firm's regulation compliance. It helps to consolidate key information about a firm's procedures. This information reveals strengths and weaknesses in the operations and supervision of agents. After the review has been completed, the checklist must be reviewed by the designated supervisor. The supervisor must attest in writing, on the member firm's letterhead stationary, that the "Self-Examination Checklist" review was completed satisfactorily.

GENERAL CHECKLIST SUBSECTIONS

Supervision: General Checklist-Supervision requires members to have a 'supervision procedures' manual that mandates the designation of a 'compliance officer' and includes directions on how to record, investigate, and respond to inquiries or complaints. It should state that branch offices must direct customer complaints to the main office and that customers should be given a list of options on how to file a claim stemming from a complaint. A firm should also have an 'Auditor' to annually audit the firms' branch offices and guaranteed IBs when they exist. The Auditor should be briefed on NFA On-Site Audit rules, should record the audit results in writing, and report to an officer of the firm.

The Member firm should take measures to correct any problems discovered by the audit. Employees should be informed of changes in rules that resulted from the audit. APs of a firm should be given training on futures and options markets and sales solicitation. Sales solicitations and mail should be monitored by a supervisor. Non customer and proprietary trading' should also be monitored by a supervisor.

Registration: General Checklist- Registration requires that Members regularly update their Form 7-R. Form 7-R should list all principals and their position, their financial relationship with the Member, and whether they have influence on the Member that is 'subject to regulation by the Commission'. Branch office locations and their managers should also be listed on Form7-R. Members should verify that Branch offices are presenting themselves as associated with the main office. Any 'doing business as' name should also be listed. It also requires that Members verify that everyone in their office, who should be registered, is registered and has met proficiency requirements. Members also must verify that APs have attended ethics training and properly handle customer accounts. All guarantee agreements, termination forms, and reportable position forms must be completed, signed, and filed with the NFA within specified deadlines.

Business Continuity and Disaster Recovery Plan: General checklist –Business continuity and Disaster Recovery Plan (hereafter the "Plan") requires a Member firm to have their Plan written. It should be periodically reviewed, tested, and revised, as needed. It should factor in business disruptions caused by third parties. Copies of the Plan should be kept off-site. The Plan should require that a computer backup of all key data kept off site, and that this data, including critical physical documents, be backed up regularly and/or copied. The backup facility should be powered by a different power grid than the one that powers the main office. Essential paper documents should be copied and stored offsite as well. The Plan should establish procedures for employees to work remotely, either from another office of from home. Employee telephone and e-mail lists should be maintained. These procedures should account for disruption of public utility services and should require cross training of employees. A communication tree should be established for emergency situations, it should include employees, board members, customers, vendors, and NFA.

Ethics Training: General checklist-Ethics Training requires Members to establish, maintain, and implement an ethics training policy. The policy should specify the frequency and duration of ethics training required for new and current registrants. It should require that the ethics trainer be qualified and have proof of their qualifications on record. Records should also be kept on a registrants' ethics training. These records should include the dates the registrant attended the ethics training, the names of the providers, and the content of training materials. Member firms should review their ethics training policy regularly and update it as needed.

Privacy Rules: General Checklist- Privacy Rules requires that a Member firm have a written privacy policy as required by CFTC Regulation 160.The Member firm must implement the policy if the customer is an individual and uses the firm's services primarily for personal or family use. Upon opening an account, and then a minimum of once per year for the duration of the account, customers must be informed of the privacy policy and the firm's 'opt out' procedures. The privacy policy must require that a customer's nonpublic (i.e. social security numbers, account numbers, trading history) personal information be kept secure, and must describe how the Member firm will secure it. It must also require disclosure to the customer which third parties, if any, will have access to their personal information.

Account Opening: General checklist- Account Opening requires that Member firms adhere to industry standards before allowing an account to be opened. Member firms must obtain sufficient customer information including name, age, occupation, annual income, net worth, and prior trading experience. If the customer declines to provide the information, the customer must submit a written document stating that they declined to provide the information. The information must be reviewed and approved by qualified supervisor of the firm. The customer's signature must be verified and, in the case of electronic signatures, protected from unauthorized use. The customer must be given a thorough risk disclosure statement by a trained individual and that individual must also be supervised by a qualified supervisor, as required by NFA Compliance Rule 2-30.

Cash flow: General checklist-Cash Flow requires that Member firms maintain accurate and regularly updated records of cash flow. To accommodate this requirement, all disbursements must be approved by responsible individuals, payments must be made by check (petty cash is excluded and does not need to be converted to check form), and a list of all cash receipts must be maintained. Branch offices must have their disbursements approved as well. Bank accounts must be authorized to be used to make disbursements and there must be documents that state this. Only authorized employees should have access to blank checks, voided checks, and signature plates used for the firm's disbursements. Before deposit, customer checks must be copied, reviewed for account/owner match, and endorsed by a qualified person.

Security Futures Products: General Checklist- Security Futures Products requires Member firms to have written procedures for employee activities involving security futures products. The procedures should include a requirement that a security futures principal be at each office, including branch offices. It should also include the requirement that the Member firm is complying with the Securities Exchange Act of 1934, specifically sections 9(a) and (b), and 10(b). It should state that any individual, who will be working with security futures, should have their most recent Form 8-T or U-5 reviewed and verified in the Central Registration Depository (CRD). APs should also complete "security futures trading training modules". Customer accounts should be reviewed to verify their financial status and suitability, and a written explanation detailing why the account was approved if the customer failed to meet securities trading requirements. Further customer information should be obtained including employment, marital, and family status. The standard disclosure and promotional material requirements should be met before security future trading is permitted by a customer.

FUTURES TRADING ROLES REQUIRED TO REGISTER WITH THE NFA

In general, any individual or firm acting in a role in which customer contact occurs for the purposes of receiving orders for futures and option contracts, executing orders for futures and option contracts, processing payments, and accounting for trading activities on behalf of customers is required to be registered with the National Futures Association (NFA). These roles include:

- futures commission merchant
- introducing broker
- commodity trading advisor
- commodity pool operator
- floor broker
- floor trader
- associated person

FLOOR BROKERS AND FLOOR TRADERS

A floor trader is an individual who conducts floor trading activities, but also acts on behalf of his or her own account. Although floor traders do not execute orders on behalf of customers, they are subject to the same registration requirements as floor brokers [National Futures Association (NFA) Registration Rule 205]. That is, they must be registered through the NFA, although they do not need to be actual members of the NFA.

ASSOCIATED PERSON

An associated person is an individual who is employed by an FCM [or associated with an introducing broker (IB), a commodity trading advisor (CTA), or a commodity pool operator (CPO)] and involved in any capacity with the solicitation or acceptance of customer orders. An associated person (AP) must be sponsored for registration by an FCM or other registrant (such as an IB, a CTA, or a CPO). The AP must provide certification of such sponsorship to the National Futures Association (NFA). A prospective AP must also satisfy the proficiency requirements of the NFA by achieving a satisfactory score on the Series 3 exam. The registration of an AP will remain valid only while he or she is employed by the sponsor.

Generally, all individuals who have contact with customers for the purpose of securing orders and all individuals in the related supervisory chain must register as associated persons (APs) with the National Futures Association (NFA). The exceptions to the AP registration requirement are as follows:

- The individual is already registered with the National Futures Association (NFA) as either a futures commission merchant (FCM), an introducing broker (IB), or a floor broker (FB).
- The individual is already registered as a commodity pool operator (CPO) in association with a CPO, unless he or she is already registered with the National Association of Securities Dealers (NASD) and futures activity is specific to the CPO only.
- The individual is already registered as a commodity trading advisor (CTA) in association with a CTA.

SOURCE FOR EXEMPTIONS FROM REGISTRATION

Generally, any individual or firm that wants to trade futures must register with the National Futures Association (NFA), unless certain exemptions apply. The governing statute to which NFA rules must conform is the Commodity Exchange Act (CEA). These rules must also comply with the regulations of the Commodity Futures Trading Commission (CFTC).

NFA RULE 2-37

NFA rule 2-37 'Security Futures Products' states that Members who are broker-dealers who carry security futures products must provide the NFA "Background Affiliation Status Information Center" (BASIC) information to security futures customers. This should be accompanied by contact information like a web site address. The NFA must be notified within 10 business days about any Member violations of NFA, SEC or CFTC rules or regulations that are in connection with security futures trading. This includes customer complaints about the Member's involvement in theft, misappropriation of funds, or forgery in connection with security futures transactions. Also if the Member is a defendant or respondent and a claim for damages has been disposed by judgment, award, or settlement in civil action, or is subject to a claim for damages and the amount exceeds $15,000, then it should be reported to NFA. NFA rule 2-37 'Security Futures Products' also states that Members should file quarterly reports with the NFA that list statistical and summary information about written customer complaints related to security futures transactions. Associates of NFA Members must promptly report additional information about any violations of NFA, SEC, or CFTC rules or regulations to their sponsors. This also includes customer complaints, theft, fraud, or any other violation. This information should be included in the quarterly reports. If no violation occurred in the quarter, then no report needs to be filed.

NFA RULE 3-1

The NFA Rule 3-1 describes, among other things, what the NFA Compliance Department does and is prohibited from doing. The Compliance Department

27

conducts an audit to investigate violations by the Member. It has the authority to compel testimony, subpoena documents, require statements under oath from any Member or their Associate and can prosecute the Member if necessary. The Compliance Department members are prohibited from being Members of the NFA. The Compliance Department members cannot trade directly or indirectly in commodities, this includes options or futures contracts. The only possible exception to this rule is if the NFA President grants approval for Compliance Department members to trade.

The NFA Rule 3-1 also describes in detail the process that is set in motion by a customer complaint, or report of a violation. After a complaint has been received or information obtained that gives reason to believe a violation has occurred, the Compliance Department prepares a report to be submitted to the BCC (Business Conduct Committee). The report includes the reason for the investigation, a summary of the complaint, if applicable, and the Compliance Department's conclusion. Investigations conducted by the Compliance Department are to be completed within 4 months.

NFA rule 3-1 also describes how the BCC (Business Conduct Committee) deals with a complaint report. When the BCC receives an investigation report it first reviews it to determine if more information or evidence is necessary to make a decision. It also must verify that none of the BCC members who are reviewing the complaint have any personal or financial affiliation with the parties involved. Members who do must refrain from reviewing the complaint. If more information is required, the BCC will request this of the Compliance Department. After 30 days of receiving the completed report, including additional information, the BCC makes a decision. It will either close the matter or serve a written, dated complaint to the Member. If the matter is closed, then the BCC must write a closure order and send this to the President. Within 10 days the order becomes final unless the President refers it to the Appeals Committee. Members of the Appeals Committee cannot have been part of any previous stage in the complaint process. The Appeals Committee then has 30 days to send it back to the BCC if it is deemed necessary.

NFA RULE 3-4

NFA rule 3-4 describes notices of charges that the Business Conduct Committee (BCC) must include in Complaint orders. Complaints must list NFA requirement(s) that have been or will be violated, and the act(s) or omission(s) that are considered in violation. Also, the NFA must inform, in writing, the respondent Member that the Member has 30 days to file a written answer to the complaint. Failure to file an answer equates to admission of guilt, acceptance of legal conclusions indicated in the complaint, and waiver of a hearing.

If there is good cause, the BCC can waive the effects of non-response, and can grant a time extension. The notice should also state that the respondent Member has a right to an attorney or other person to represent them at any stage of the investigation.

NFA RULE 3-8

NFA rule 3-8 describes the Respondents opportunity to review the complaint during a pre-hearing. Any information or evidence that the Compliance Department is using to make their decision can be viewed simultaneously by the Member who is considered to be possibly in violation. The Respondent Member must request the material in writing, and must state where they would like to examine the material; either at NFA offices or the respondent Member's offices. In the later case, the material must be copied and sent to the Respondent at the Respondent's expense. Privileged information might be withheld. The Chairman of the Hearing Panel will schedule times and locations, and provide technology required for viewing and/ or conferencing (i.e. telephone conferences).

NFA RULE 3-9 AND 3-10

NFA rules 3-9 and 3-10 on 'Hearing' describes what is permitted if/when a hearing is held. The Hearing panel oversees the hearing. Members of the panel cannot be personally or financially associated with any of the participants (see Bylaw 708(c)). Formal rules of evidence are not necessary. The Respondent can appear personally, and can call and examine any witnesses. They can present evidence and relevant testimony. Telephone testimony can be permitted. Also, any party involved can request that other persons connected with the matter be ordered to testify or produce documents .The Hearing Panel can use discretion when granting the request. If it is granted, the testimony will be paid for by the party requesting it. After the hearing, the Heating Panel writes a decision that must include the evidence, charges, the answer, a statement of conclusions of each allegation, each penalty imposed, the penalty dates, and notice that the respondent has 15 days to appeal the decisions. The decision is signed and given to the Respondent and Appeals committee. It becomes final after the 15 days expire.

NFA RULE 3-11

NFA Rule 3-11 describes the settlement process. The Respondent can submit their proposed settlement to the BCC (Business Conduct Committee), BCC panel, Hearing Panel, or Appeals Committee, depending on what stage the hearing is in. The settlement offer can include the statement that the Respondent neither admits nor denies guilt. However, the NFA requires that every settlement offer must include certain language, depending on which group the offer has been submitted to ; BCC or BCC Panel, Hearing Panel, Appeals committee, or the Compliance Department (The specific language for each group can be found in Rule 3-ll). The required language basically ensures that the Respondent knows who will receive the offer next, in the event the offer is rejected. Also, it ensures that the Respondent knows that the offer is nullified upon final rejection.

Rule 3-11 also describes the content of the written and dated appeals statement decision. It clarifies again that Appeals Committee members can't be part of the decision if they have been part of any previous stage of the complaint process (with the exception of the settlement review). The decision should include the conclusions of each charge and penalty, the basis for that particular penalty, and the date the penalty should begin to take effect. It should also state that anyone who will suffer from the penalty can either petition to postpone the penalty start date within 10 days, or appeal it within 30 days (Commission Regulations part 171). The decision is final after 30 days.

NFA RULE3-14

NFA rule 3-14 Penalties describes the possible penalties that could be imposed on a Respondent as a disciplinary action. The Respondent could be expelled or just suspended for a period of time, from NFA membership. Expulsion requires 2/3 vote. Suspension withholds membership rights (i.e. calling themselves an NFA Member, trading, accepting new accounts etc.) from the Member, but requires the responsibilities to be maintained (i.e. dues, assessments, etc.) during the suspension period. The Respondent could be prohibited from association with other Members, ordered to take remedial action (i.e. increase their capital or capital requirements), ordered to cease all trading activity, or be fined a maximum of $250,000 per violation. Any fines imposed must be paid within 30 days of decision, to the NFA Treasurer. Failure to pay the fine on time could lead to suspension or a restriction against association with other Members.

NFA RULE 802
IMPLICATIONS OF FILING FORM 7-R

NFA Registration Rule 802 describes the implication of form 7-R. Registration of FCMs, IBs, CPOs, and CTAs requires that Form 7-R be electronically filed with the NFA. When filing this form, the applicant is certifying that the person filing the form is authorized to do so and that the information is true, complete, accurate and current. If it is not, the applicant accepts the possible resulting criminal penalties. The applicant will not act as if the application itself grants registration or Temporary License, and all the associated rights of Membership.

The applicant also grants NFA right to investigate the applicant, including questioning foreign regulatory or law enforcement agencies about the applicant, and obtaining official personal documents to determine the applicant's fitness. The applicant also agrees that the parties providing the information about the applicant are not held liable for providing the information.

EXEMPTIONS

Registration Rule 802 also states that Form 7-R implies certain conditions if the applicant is applying for exemption from registration as an IB, CPO, or CTA.(see CFTC Regulation 30.5) .In this case, the applicant agrees to not act as any of these designations in connection with trading in the US, on behalf of US customers. The applicant accepts that the Commission and federal courts have jurisdiction over any of their activities that are subject to CFTC regulations. Also, the applicant confirms that it is not disqualified from registration because of laws of their own country.

FOREIGN APPLICANTS

NFA Registration Rule 802 also implies conditions if applicant to NFA is foreign. Foreign applicants agree to permit the CFTC, the U.S. Justice Department, and NFA to inspect the applicant's books and records to determine compliance with all requirements. It also requires copies of any audits or reports about the foreign applicant issued by non-US regulatory agencies. The foreign applicant has 72 hours after the request to produce the information at the specified location. Only 24 hours is permitted if the foreign applicant is applying for registration as an FCM. Any changes to the location must be reported immediately to the NFA. Failure to comply with these conditions could result in disciplinary actions against the foreign applicant.

REQUIREMENTS OF FBS AND FTS

The Registration rule 802 states requirements for FBs (Floor Brokers) or FTs (Floor Traders). The electronic filing of a Form 8-R for registration as an FB or FT implies certain conditions of the applicant. It implies that the applicant certifies that the information in Form 8-R is true, complete (no omissions), current, and not misleading in any way. The applicant also confirms that the business address listed in Form 8-R is the location to send any written information from the NFA or Commission. If the Business address should change, or another delivery location (i.e. attorney's office) for legal documents (i.e. subpoena, summons, arbitration claims etc.) is established, then this information should be entered into the electronic Form 8-R promptly. The applicant agrees to be subject to possible criminal penalties for false statements or omissions made in Form 8.

The Registration Rule 802 also states what FBs (Floor Brokers) and FTs (Floor Traders) are subject to by filing Form 8-R. They are basically the same conditions that exist with the filing of Form 7-R. The applicant grants the NFA the right to investigate the applicant to determine fitness for membership, and agrees to cooperate with the investigation. Foreign authorities may be contacted, official documents may be obtained, and persons providing the information must not be held liable for damages that might result from providing the information. The act of applying for registration implies that the applicant is not registered, and therefore may not act as an FB or FT until registration or TL (Temporary License) is granted.

REQUIREMENTS FOR APS AND THEIR SPONSORS

Registration Rule 802 requires the electronic filing of Form 8-R on behalf of APs (Associated Persons) and implies that the applicant agrees to certain terms. The applicant certifies that the statements in Form 8-R are true, complete, accurate and current and that the person completing the form was authorized to do so. It also states that the AP applicant has authorized the sponsor to file Form 8-R on behalf of the AP. It is implied that the sponsor has communicated, when possible, with all previous employers and educational institutions of the applicant from the past 3 years. The sponsor should have documentation of these contacts. Also, it is implied that the sponsor has hired or intends to hire the applicant, to act as an AP, within 30 days after registration or TL (Temporary License) has been granted. However, the applicant will not act as an AP until such registration has actually been granted. The sponsor also confirms, by filing Form 8-R, that the applicant is not subject to disqualification from registration, and that the sponsor meets all requirements as well.

NFA Registration rule 802 requires electronic filing of Form 8-R and implies that the applicant for registration as AP is providing accurate, complete, and current information.

It implies that the residential address provided on the Form 8-R is the correct address for delivery of any written information from the NFA or Commission. This written information can include notices that would affect the applicant's registration or status as principal, so it is very important that the applicant's address information is kept current. If an alternate address is used for legal documents, that address should also be listed on Form 8-R. Of course, it is implied that the applicant will maintain whatever address is listed on Form 8-R while registered as an AP or Principal. It must also be maintained for 2 years after the termination of the registration. The applicant for AP also agrees to submit to the same jurisdiction, rules, and regulations as that of their sponsor.

PENALTIES FOR APS WHEN FALSELY FILING FORM 8-R

Registration Rule 802 requires the electronic filing of Form 8-R on behalf of an AP (Associated Person) by their sponsor. And implies that the applicant is aware of the penalties they are subject to. They are similar to the penalties described in Form 7-R. The applicant acknowledges that they are subject to criminal penalties for false statements and omissions. Even though it is the AP who is the applicant, it is the sponsor of the AP who is responsible for maintaining Form 8-R by submitting electronic updates. The sponsor also agrees that they must verify that the potential AP is not disqualified from registration for any reason, and must notify the Commission if that changes. The sponsor also acknowledges their responsibility for supervising the AP in an effort to prevent violations by the AP.

APPLYING FOR A TL

NFA Registration Rule 802 requires the electronic filing of Form 8-R when applying for a TL. Completing Form 8-R implies certain certifications. It implies that the sponsor has obtained, from the NFA's BASIC system, all information concerning the applicant. This includes any pending actions against the applicant and any actions that resulted in the withdrawal of the individual's application within the last 12 months. The sponsor should retain copies of the notices for these pending actions. If the applicant's registration can only be granted under certain conditions, the sponsor also agrees, through the filing of Form 8-R, to meet those conditions. This includes supervising the applicant as required by the NFA regulations.

SECURITIES EXCHANGE ACT OF 1934
MAIN OBJECTIVE

The main objective of the Securities Exchange Act of 1934 was to create a body to oversee company compliance with the Securities Act of 1933.This body was called the Securities and Exchange Commission. It was granted authority over the securities industry, including brokerage, clearing and transfer firms, the stock exchanges, and all the national SROs (Self-Regulatory Organizations) including FINRA. This Commission is charged with registering, regulating, and disciplining the securities industry members. For example, anytime shareholders are asked to vote on a company action, the solicitation information provided them, must first be submitted to the SEC to verify compliance with disclosure requirements. Shareholder groups must also first submit any information they intend to provide shareholders, to the SEC for review. The SEC can delegate those duties to the SROs or exchanges. In fact, the SEC requires that Exchanges and SROs have rules that will effectively discourage improper conduct of its members.

PROHIBITED BEHAVIOR

In addition to requiring regular reports by public companies, this Act also defines prohibited behavior related to securities trading. Attempts to gain control of a publicly traded company is prohibited unless disclosure information, including intent and other important information, is first submitted to the SEC. Attempting to acquire more than 5% of a company's stock is usually considered an effort to gain control of a company. This gives the shareholders an opportunity to make informed decisions about their investment. Also, insider trading is strictly prohibited and frequently the reason for disciplinary action. Specifically, insider trading is illegal when someone who is required to withhold certain information or is prohibited from trading, uses the non-public information to trade anyway.

MAIN OBJECTIVE OF THE SECURITIES ACT OF 1933

The Securities Act of 1933, also known as the "truth in securities" law, has two main objectives. They are to ensure that investors are given adequate information about a security and the company offering it, and to ensure that the information not be fraudulent.

These goals were obtained by requiring that securities, with some exceptions, be registered. The registration "statement and prospectus" must describe a company's management, product or services, and properties. It must also include independently certified financial statements of the company. All this information is first examined for compliance, and then made available to the public via the SEC's EDGAR database. The exceptions to this rule include limited (less than 500 owners), private offerings, intrastate offerings, and local and federal government offerings.

CFTC AND THE SEC

The CFTC (Commodity Futures Trading Commission) and SEC (Securities Exchange Commission) are federal regulatory agencies whose commissioners are appointed by the President, with confirmation by the Senate. The CFTC was created as a result of the Commodity Futures Trading Commission Act, which was amended in 1974. It is comprised of five commissioners and oversees all futures trading in the United States. It is not dependent on any cabinet departments. The CFTC required a Designated Self Regulatory Organization (DSRO) be established to monitor

33

commodity traders. That organization is the National Futures Association (NFA). Its responsibilities are to enforce standards through audits and monitoring of NFA Members. The SEC was created by the SEC Act of 1934 to govern all aspects of the securities industry.

MARKETS WITHIN THE TRADING INDUSTRY

There are various kinds of markets within the trading industry, as well as specialized products that require specific permission to trade. The general term to describe the regulated cash trading markets is "Over the Counter Market". It is where stocks, foreign currencies, other cash items are bought and sold via telephone or other electronic communication. The Foreign Exchange Market (Forex) conducts foreign exchange business by telephone or other electronic methods. The CBOT requires its Members to become qualified to trade in the government instrument market (GIM) category, which trades in local and federal government financial instruments. The CBOT also requires its' Members become qualified to trade futures contracts in the index, debt, and energy markets category (IDEM). This includes "gold, municipal bond index, 30 day fed funds, and stock index futures".

ELECTRONIC REPORTING SYSTEMS USED IN THE COMMODITIES TRADING INDUSTRY

To comply with the numerous CFTC rules and regulations, the commodities trading industry requires constant, thorough self-reporting. To facilitate this reporting, several electronic reporting systems have been developed by various exchanges and other entities:

- CTRS (Computerized Trading Reconstruction System)-The CBOT (Chicago Board Of Trade) has an electronic surveillance program that can the characteristics of any trade, including the specific contract, quantity, price, and time of execution to the nearest minute.
- MIDIS (Market Information Data Inquiry System) - This data base has all of the historical CBOT information about price volume, open interest and other market information.
- LDB (Liquidity Data Bank) – This data bank gives a profile of market activity on the CBOT. It can display price trends, daily volume data, and time distribution of prices for every commodity. A Market Profile can be ordered for a particular commodity. The CBOT also has an electronic price-reporting system that can provide critical pricing data. Traders use this information to analyze markets and price trends.
- FACTS (Financial Analysis Auditing Compliance Tracking System)-The NFA also has an electronic system for maintenance of financial records of its Members. It also monitors their current financial condition.
- GLOBEX – GLOBEX is a global after-hours electronic trading system.

BEAR AND BULL STRATEGIES

The difference between the current cash price and the futures price of the same commodity in a nearby month (the month closest to expiration) is called the basis. The basis helps determine a trader's strategy. If they trader thinks the prices will decline relative to the basis of a commodity, then the trader is a bear, and will act as though the market was a bear market. Bears will try to profit from a bear market by using a strategy called a bear spread. This means they will sell the nearby contract month and buy the deferred contract month, and profit from the difference in prices. The opposite strategy is used by bulls, those who believe prices will rise. In a bull market, bulls will buy the nearby contract month and sell the deferred contract month. The profit also comes from the price difference.

RESTRICTIONS CUSTOMERS CAN PUT ON TRADING ORDERS

A customer can set restrictions on their orders, with which their trader must comply. A limit order is an order that has a limit on the price and/or time of execution. The expression 'fill or kill' is used to describe what must be done with a price limit order. It means to fill the order or cancel it. A stop order is an order to buy or sell at a *set* price. A stop order to buy is exercised when the futures contract trades (are bid) at or above the stop price. A stop order to sell is exercised when the futures contract trades (are offered) at or below the stop price.

A stop-limit order is similar to a stop order. If the order cannot be executed at the exact price or better, the order is not executed. It is held until the stated price is reached again. A time-limit order specifies a time when the order can be executed.

A canceling order deletes a previous order.

SPECULATOR AND HEDGER

A speculator differs from a hedger in that a speculator does not produce or need the underlying commodity of a futures contract. Their goal is to profit from the price differences that arise in the market. They assume the risk that the hedgers do not want. Even though, hedgers will sometimes act as speculators, speculators will rarely assume the role of hedgers. Speculators enable the liquidity of markets that makes for efficient flow of trade. Therefore, their role in the commodities industry is very important.

CARRYING CHARGE

Some physical commodities, like grain or oilseed, are not always completely consumed during the market year. These physical products must be kept in storage. These stocks are 'carried over' to, or counted as part of, the next marketing year. A carrying charge, or cost of carry, is charged on this storage. It includes the physical costs of storing the commodities as well as the insurance and finance charges that are related to the storage. A carrying charge can also apply to interest rate futures. For interest rate charges, the carrying charge is the difference between yield on the cash instrument and the cost of funds used to buy the instrument.

OPEN INTEREST, VOLATILITY, AND VOLUME

To offset a *purchase* of futures contracts, an equal amount of futures contracts of the same commodity are *sold*. To offset a *sale* of futures contracts, an equal amount of futures contracts of the same commodity are *bought*. Open Interest describes the total number of futures or options contracts that have not yet been offset by an opposite transaction, nor fulfilled by delivery. Each open transaction has a buyer and seller, but only one side of the contract is counted when calculating open interest. In addition to the open interest calculations, volatility and volume help to analyze price trends. Volatility describes the change in price of a commodity over a given time span. It is the annualized standard deviation of the percentage change in daily price. Volume describes the number of purchases or sales of a commodity futures contract made during a specific time span.

FEED RATIO

Fair commodity prices can be figured by using various ratios. The Feed Ratio is used to describe the relationship between feeding costs and the value of livestock. For example, a hog/corn ratio refers to the hog feeding cost as it relates to the monetary value of the hog. To derive the hog corn ratio, divide the hog price by the corn price. The hog price is based on price per hundred pounds. The corn price is based on price per bushel. When corn prices are high compared to hog prices, then it will take fewer units of corn to equal the value of 100 pounds of hog. This information will help determine what commodity should be bought or sold.

TERMS USED IN COMMODITY CONTRACTS

Commodities are products like metals, petroleum, foreign currencies, and financial instruments and, of course, agricultural. These are all products that can be traded on an authorized commodity exchange. Generally, they have different contract grades (or deliverable grades) and time spans.

If the quality of a commodity differs from the contract grade, then a schedule of allowable discounts or premiums is used to determine its price.

The contract time span from harvest to harvest is the Crop Year (or Marketing Year). It varies with the commodity. For example, the marketing year for soybeans is from September 1 to August 31. So for futures contracts, November is the first major new-crop month and July is the last major old-crop month for soybeans.

A warehouse receipt documents the existence and availability of a given commodity in storage. It is often used to transfer ownership in cash and futures transactions.

NUMBER OF ARBITRATORS ON A PANEL

The NFA has arbitration rules that apply to NFA Members when a non-Member customer files a complaint about a Member FCM, IB, CTA, CPO, or LTM, or any of their employees. These rules are in effect when arbitration is required by legal agreement. For claims less than $50,000, an arbitration panel composed of just one arbitrator will be assigned. If the claim exceeds $50,000, a panel composed of three arbitrators will be assigned. The exception to this is if the claim is between $25,000 and $50,000, but one of the participants requests three arbitrators. This panel will determine an award, if any, within thirty days of the closing of record. The written decision will be submitted to the Secretary who sends copies to all participants.

ARBITRABLE DISPUTES

In general, arbitration procedures are mandatory in situations where there is a dispute between a National Futures Association (NFA) member and a customer. In order for a dispute brought forth by a customer against a member or member associate to be arbitrable, the following three conditions must be met:

- The customer cannot be a futures commission merchant (FCM), a floor broker (FB), an NFA member, or an associated person (AP).
- The nexus of the dispute cannot involve cash market transactions that do not have a direct relationship to a futures transaction.
- The respondent NFA member or associate must be a futures commission merchant (FCM), a retail foreign exchange dealer (RFED), an introducing broker (IB), a commodity pool operator (CPO), a commodity trading advisor (CTA), or a leverage transaction merchant (LTM).

THIRD PARTY CLAIMS

A third party claim (filed by a respondent against a party not subject to the proceedings) may be filed if the claim has arisen out of an act or a transaction that is the subject of the arbitration claim.

ARBITRATION PANEL

The secretary of the National Futures Association (NFA) is responsible for appointing an arbitration panel to adjudicate dispute proceedings. Arbitration panel members must be NFA members or individuals associated with NFA members. The criteria for determining the size of an arbitration panel are as follows:

- For claims not greater than $100,000, the panel consists of a single panel member.
- For claims greater than $100,000, the panel consists of three panel members.
- For claims between $50,000 and not more than $100,000, an additional two members may be appointed upon the request of all parties involved.

TIME FRAME FOR FILING AN ARBITRATION CLAIM

An arbitration claim or notice of intent to arbitrate must be filed in order for a dispute to be arbitrable with the National Futures Association (NFA). An arbitration claim or notice of intent to arbitrate must be filed with the NFA within two years of the date on which the claimant became aware or should have become aware that an arbitrable dispute existed.

FILING ANSWERS TO CLAIMS

Once an arbitration claim has been filed, the National Futures Association (NFA) will initiate the proceedings by notifying each person named on the claim as a respondent. Answers must be filed by the respondent within the time periods below:

- for claims not exceeding $50,000, 20 days from the date of service of the claim by the NFA
- for claims greater than $50,000 but not exceeding $100,000, 45 days from the date of service of the claim by the NFA
- for claims greater than $100,000, 45 days from the date of service of the claim by the NFA

INDIVIDUALS AUTHORIZED TO ACT AS COUNSEL

Parties to an arbitration proceeding held before the National Futures Association (NFA) are entitled to be assisted by counsel. What individuals are authorized to act as counsel? Any party to such a dispute may be represented by:

- an attorney
- a non-compensated family member who has no vested interest in the outcome of the dispute
- an officer, partner, or employee of the party

HEARING PLAN

During the pre-hearing phase of an arbitration proceeding held before the National Futures Association (NFA), the parties are expected to cooperate by exchanging all relevant documents and jointly contributing to the preparation of a hearing plan. A hearing plan is a document that summarizes each claim, each answer to a claim, and each reply to an answer. The document also includes:

- the factual and legal issues pertaining to the dispute
- a list of witnesses and exhibits that will be presented at the hearing

DISMISSING A CLAIM

A panel may dismiss a claim either of its own initiative or at the request of one or both of the parties if it determines that the claim is not a proper subject for NFA arbitration. This determination is made at the panel's discretion.

SUMMARY HEARING

An arbitration panel hearing is scheduled by the secretary of the National Futures Association (NFA). At the designated time, the parties are afforded the opportunity to appear, testify, and present evidence before the panel. A hearing can be conducted using written material only (i.e., a summary hearing) in the following three circumstances. The secretary of the panel must also agree to conduct a summary hearing.

- The amount of the claims in aggregate does not exceed $25,000.
- The amount of the claims in aggregate is greater than $25,000, but does not exceed $50,000, and one of the parties requests an oral hearing.
- Both parties request a summary hearing and the panel agrees to waive an oral hearing.

MODIFICATION OF AWARDS

Generally, decisions by the arbitration panel of the National Futures Association (NFA) and any related awards are considered to be final and binding on the parties. Typically, the parties do not have a right to appeal. After the final judgment, an award may be modified in the following circumstances when a written request is made by one of the parties within 20 days of the date of service of the award:

- The award was based on a material calculation error or on an improper description of any person, thing, or property relevant to the award.
- The award was based on a matter not properly referred to the panel.
- The award is imperfect in matter of form.

ARBITRATION COSTS

Arbitration costs required by the National Futures Association (NFA) are the responsibility of the claimant. A panel may assess reasonable and necessary expenses against a respondent if the panel finds the respondent engaged in willful acts of bad faith or presented a frivolous defense. Attorney fees may also be assessed in situations where this is legally permitted.

INITIATION OF DISCIPLINARY PROCEEDINGS DURING ARBITRATION OR MEDIATION

When disputes are submitted to arbitration or mediation, the NFA retains the right to initiate a disciplinary proceeding at its discretion.

CLEARINGHOUSE

A cash market is a place, like a grain elevator or a bank, where actual commodities are bought and sold. Spot refers to the cash price for the immediately available commodity. A forward contract is a private, non- standardized cash contract to exchange the physical commodities. A futures contract is a standardized contract that is publicly traded on commodities exchanges. These futures contracts require some third party to settle trading accounts on a daily basis. This is the responsibility of a clearinghouse. A clearinghouse settles and clears trades, collects and maintains margin funds, and regulates physical delivery. It acts as a third party to all futures and options contracts, by being the buyer for every sale and the seller to every buyer.

CHARACTERISTICS TO DETERMINE PARTICIPATION ELIGIBILITY

Many prospective customers of futures trading do not have the psychological ability to withstand the peculiar risks inherent to commodities trading. Investing in securities is not quite the same in terms of extreme volatility and amount of leverage available. Therefore, Members are required to assess the suitability of the personality of a potential customer to futures trading. Even though financial status is extremely important in assessing suitability, it is not necessarily sufficient for trading in futures if the individual is unwilling to risk losing it all.

Some characteristics that are considered when determining participation eligibility are:

- tolerance for severe loss, including all invested principal
- tolerance for long term fund allocation
- net worth
- current tax liability and ability to pay substantial taxes

Occasionally, there is some overlap between securities and futures trading, especially when futures trading funds are set up in a limited partnership. In this case, the rules of both the SEC and CFTC govern the trading.

RANDOM AND UNANNOUNCED ON-SITE INSPECTIONS

The frequency and duration of on-site inspections of branch offices and guaranteed IBs depends on the size of the operation. Smaller operations could have all their records and procedures inspected thoroughly in the time between visits. Larger operations typically allow for only a sample of the records and procedures to be reviewed during the time between visits. In this case, the sample choices should be randomly picked, and the visits should be random and unannounced. The results of on-site visits should be written and discussed with regional managers.

ON-SITE VISITS OF BRANCH OFFICES

The NFA requires that Members conduct annual on-site inspections of their branch offices, and the offices of their guaranteed IBs. However, the frequency of the inspections really depends on the subject office. The Member should establish set criteria for increased visits and compile a list of duties to be performed during on-site visits. It should be established when unannounced visits are necessary. This depends on the volume of business, the previous training of the officers, the frequency of customer complaints, and the kinds of problems that occur at a particular office. The personnel who conduct the on-site inspections should be very knowledgeable about the industry in general and the specialization of the particular office. The inspector should also be independent, objective and technically qualified to conduct on-site inspections.

REVIEW OF CUSTOMER ORDERS

On-site inspections of branch offices and the offices of IBs should include the review of customer order procedures. The names of anyone accepting customer orders should be written and one of their order tickets should be selected as an example for review. Order tickets should be pre-numbered. The inspector should randomly check that this is true of the order tickets. The tickets should be time stamped and all required information is included, such as name of customer, commodity, quantity, quality, and any other instructions. Option order tickets should be given particular attention, since they require additional information, as specified by CFTC Regulation 1.35.

REVIEW OF CUSTOMER DEPOSITS

On-site inspection of branch offices and guaranteed IBs should include the review of customer deposits. It should be confirmed that the office is authorized to accept customer deposits. If they are, then any customer checks or other deposit instruments should be copied before depositing them in the branch office bank account. A sample of the copies should be examined to verify that the funds are made payable to the FCM. Third party checks should also be examined to verify that a customer is really acting as an unregistered FCM or CPO. Finally, records should be examined to verify that funds are being correctly forwarded and/or transmitted in a timely manner. The customer account should be accurately credited.

REVIEW OF SALES SOLICITATION AND PROMOTIONAL MATERIALS

Sales solicitation practices and promotional materials that are used by the branch office or guaranteed IB should also be reviewed during an on-site visit. The person(s) supervising sales in the office should be qualified and registered. It should be confirmed that any person(s) responsible for making sales solicitations are registered. Their sales solicitations should be monitored during the on-site visit. The sales scripts and any other supporting promotional material used should be reviewed for accuracy and prior approval. A few customers should be interviewed about the sales process they experienced. They should be asked how their account was handled, if there were any problems, and how any complaints were handled. It should be confirmed that any customer complaints were reported to the main office.

REVIEW OF PROPRIETARY ACCOUNTS

On-site inspections of branch offices and guaranteed IBs should also include a review of proprietary account activity. Proprietary accounts are those that belong to the firm. Trading is for the direct benefit of the firm with firm funds. Persons handling proprietary account orders should have duties that are separate from the duties of persons handling customer account orders. This is to minimize exchange of sensitive non-public information that could result in trading abuses. Principals also should not be trading for their own account when they are also trading for customer's accounts.

LEVERAGE USED IN FUTURES TRADING

In futures trading, leverage is when a trader uses a small amount of money to control a much greater amount of money. For example, when a trader buys a futures contract with only 10 % margin, leverage is being used because the trader has control(and is also liable for) the remaining 90% of that contract. If the trader buys a wheat contract with a 10% margin at $5.00 per bushel, then he controls $25,000 ($5 x 5000 bushels) with just $2500. If wheat prices rise 60 cents per bushel, the trader gains $3000, 120% of the original investment. Of course if wheat prices fall by 60 cents, then 120% of the original investment is lost. These low margins contribute to the regular use of leverage in the futures industry.

BONA FIDE HEDGE

For the purpose of merchandising cash positions, the CFTC recognizes certain transactions as bona fide hedging transaction. These are futures contracts that are meant to be a substitute for the physical commodity that will be bought or sold at some future date. It relates to the assets that will be produced, processed, or merchandised by a commercial enterprise. The main purpose of a bona fide hedge is to offset price risks associated with commercial cash market operations. The value of the transactions is limited to the anticipated net cash market value that will occur within the next 12 months. Positions in a particular futures delivery month can't be held during the last 5 trading days.

SPECULATIVE POSITION LIMITS AND POSITION ACCOUNTABILITY LIMITS

Speculative position limits represent the maximum position of combined futures and options (either net long or net short) that may be held by any single trader or group of traders acting in concert. CFTC regulations currently apply such limits to grains, the soybean complex, and cotton. Exchanges may extend the limits to other commodities.

Position accountability limits permit traders to accumulate positions that exceed the limitation amounts in exchange for on-demand reporting of such positions as requested by the CFTC and/or the exchange.

EXEMPTIONS PROVIDED TO BONA FIDE HEDGERS

A speculative position limit sets the maximum value a single trader can hold in a single futures or option contract, regardless of whether the position is net short or net long. Hedge positions which conform to the structure defined by the Commodity Futures Trading Commission (CFTC) are generally exempt from position reporting limits. While the defined structure can be quite specific, the general requirements for a qualifying hedge are that the hedge:

- represents a substitute for transactions made or to be made, or for positions taken or to be taken at a later time in a physical marketing channel
- is economically appropriate for the purpose of reducing risk related to the conduct and management of a commercial enterprise
- arises from the potential change of one or several underlying assets

Monthly Statements FCMs Are Required to Submit to Customers

At the close of the last day of each month FCMs are required to submit to each commodity or option customer their monthly statements in writing. The exception to this requirement is if/when there has been no change to the account balance and there are no open positions. In that case, a statement should be submitted every three months. The statement for futures customers should include:

1. Customer funds with the FCM
2. Open contracts with their purchase prices
3. Net unrealized profits/losses for all open contracts
4. All charges and credits, funds received or disbursed, and realized profits/losses

Daily Recording Requirements of FCMs

All NFA Members are required to keep accurate and current records of their transactions and must make them available for inspection by any of the industry's regulatory bodies. The specific daily requirements for an FCM include computations of the day's transactions, which must be conducted at the close of each business day. They must be completed before noon of the following business day. The total customer funds on deposit and the total funds that CFTC regulations require to be on deposit should be computed each day. Also, the FCM's residual interest in the customer funds must also be computed each day.

Monthly Statements FCMs Are Required to Submit to Option Customers

At the close of the last day of each month FCMs are required to submit to each option customer their monthly statements in writing. The exception to this requirement is if/when there has been no change to the account balance and there are no open positions. In that case, a statement should be submitted every three months. The monthly statement for options customers should include:

1. All open option positions and their underlying futures contract, strike price, transaction and expiration date
2. All open option positions marked to the market and how much each is in-the-money
3. All options, along with their underlying futures description, sold, purchased, exercised, or expired during the month
4. All charges and credits, funds received or disbursed , and realized profits/losses

Additional Risk Disclosure

NFA's Rule 2-30 requires that Members obtain financial, personal, and business information about customers in order to determine the appropriate risk disclosure for that customer. However, for some customers, the only adequate risk disclosure is simply that futures trading is just too risky for them. Once all risk disclosure is provided, however, then the customer is ultimately free to choose if they still want to trade, and the Member is free to accept their money and open an account for them. This rule recognizes that determining levels of risk disclosure can only be done on a case by case basis, and best done by the Member, but still subject to BCC review. However, the most common violation of the rule is not that too much risk disclosure was provided, but rather that not enough was provided. Another common violation is that customers are encouraged to give false information, especially regarding their lack of futures trading or investment experience.

TERMINATION OF NFA MEMBERSHIP

Termination of NFA membership can occur in a variety of ways.

1. A temporary license could expire without the granting of membership. The NCFE must be passed.
2. If a Member defaults on their dues payments membership could be terminated.
3. A Member could resign from their NFA membership.
4. A Member could fail to renew their NFA registration.
5. A Member could terminate the employment of an AP. This termination will apply to NFA Membership if the AP does not join another Member firm within 60 days.

INFORMAL NATURE OF PARTS OF NFA COMPLIANCE RULE-30

Certain parts of the NFA's Compliance Rule -30 are not specific and were developed with consideration for a case by case basis. There is no grid like formula for APs to use to determine when additional information should be given to customers. However, Rule 2-30 does require that Members compile key determining factors to help APs identify when customers need more information. These factors should be explained to the AP., and the AP should be required to consider these factors when determining if more risk disclosure is needed. Examples of a violation of the NFA's compliance rule 2-30 would be failure of an AP to obtain the required customer information. Another example would be an AP's failure to follow the firm's procedures for determining when additional risk disclosure is needed.

These violations have not been the sole reason for disciplinary action. As case law develops in this area, the NFA will keep Members informed of any Rule application changes.

NFA CRITERIA TO DETERMINE REQUIREMENT OF EXTRA SUPERVISORY PROCEDURES

In an effort to minimize the repeated use of improper sales tactics, the NFA has established a set of criteria to determine when a Member will be required to impose extra supervisory procedures on its sales force. These criteria are:

1. Two or more of a firm's APs (when there are less than 5 APs employed at the firm) have been employed by another Member firm that has been disciplined by NFA, CFTC, SEC or any securities industry SRO for sales practice fraud (Disciplined Firm.)
2. Forty percent of a firm's APs (when there are 5-10 APS at a firm) have been employed by a Disciplined Firm.

3. Four or more of a firm's APs (when there are 10-20 APs at a firm) have been employed by a Disciplined Firm.
4. Twenty percent of a firm's APs (when there are more than 20 APs at a firm) have been employed by a Disciplined Firm.

*An exception to these criteria applies if the AP was only employed by the Disciplined Firm for less than 60 days, and has not been with a Disciplined Firm for the last 5 years

IDENTIFICATION OF PROBLEM AREAS IN A MEMBER FIRM

The NFA has developed a set of factors that would help identify potential problem areas in Member firms. These factors are based on the careful review of Member firms that were closed for deceptive sales practices. One significant factor common to the closed firms was the employment history and training of their sales force. Most of the sales force had previously worked for a Member firm that had been closed for fraud. The NFA has concluded that if a Member firm is closed for fraud related to its telemarketing or promotional materials, then it is reasonable to state that its training and supervision of its sales force is inadequate or inappropriate. It is also probable that APs, who had worked for a firm that was closed for fraud, have learned improper sales tactics. Consequently, those APs will require retraining and extra supervision if hired.

EXTRA SUPERVISORY PROCEDURE

If a firm is determined to be a Disciplined Firm, then the NFA requires the firm to be subject to extra supervisory procedures. One example of an extra supervisory procedure is the requirement that all telephone conversations between an AP and customers or potential customers be recorded. These recordings should be labeled with the date and name of AP, be catalogued, be kept for five years from the date of recording and be readily available for 2 years. In addition, APs are required to keep a daily log of all customers and potential customers they spoke with each day. These daily written logs must also be catalogued and kept for five years.

NFA CRITERIA FOR DETERMINING A "DISCIPLINED FIRM"

The NFA has established criteria for when firms are considered to be a "Disciplined Firm".

1. The firm has been formally charged with deceptive telemarketing practices or fraudulent promotional material, by the CFTC or the NFA.
2. The formal charges against the firm have been resolved and resulted in the firm being permanently barred from the industry.
3. The firm has been disciplined because of deceptive sales practices involving securities.
4. A dealer-broker that has been expelled from security industry membership or has had their broker-dealer registration revoked by the SEC.

PARTIAL FILL IN BUNCHED ORDERS

In futures trading bunched orders are when a trader places orders for multiple accounts at the same time. For example, a CTA might place a bunched order of 200 contracts for multiple accounts, and the contracts might be filled at different prices. Sometimes, the bunched order is to be filled at a specific price. This creates problems if the CTAs' FCM is not being able to execute all of the 200 contracts (lot order, or bunched order) at that price. This is known as a partial fill. An FCM should be given guidelines by the CTA on how to fairly fill bunched orders.

ALLOCATION METHODS FOR BUNCHED ORDERS

For bunched orders, Random Allocation of contracts is when firms use a computer program to randomly select and order the participating account numbers. The program allocates the best price to the account numbers first on the list. The least favorable price would be allocated to the account that is last on the list. The remaining allocations are rotated as in the Rotation method of allocation. The Highest Price to Highest Account numbers is another allocation method for bunched orders. It is self-descriptive. In theory, this method is equitable because the high numbered accounts that get best price on the sell order will have their advantage offset by the less favorable price on the buy order. This method does not always result in fairness. However, it is consistent enough to be an acceptable allocation method.

SPECIFIC FEES INCLUDED IN A BREAK EVEN ANALYSIS

A sample break-even report is shown below, and lists all the fees and expenses that should be included in any break even analysis. The percentages indicated in this sample may vary from actual percentages:

1. Selling price per unit (initial) - $1,000.00
2. Syndication and Selling Expense (specific contracted rate) - $50.00
3. General Partner's Management Fee (specific contracted rate) -$9.50
4. Fund Operating Expenses (accounting, auditing, and legal expenses of the account. Usually about 2% of the Net asset value of the fund) - $20.50
5. Trading Advisor's and Trading Manager's Management fees(a combined monthly fee equal to about .0016 of the funds allocated net assets)- $28.50
6. Trading Advisor's and Trading Manager's Incentive Fees and Trading Profits (a percentage of trading profits) - $17.17
7. Brokerage Commissions and Trading Fees (about 4% of Net Asset Value) - $38
8. Less Interest Income (7) – ($28.50)
9. Amount of Trading Income Required for the Fund's Net Asset Value per Unit (Redemption Value) at the End of One Year to Equal the Selling Price per Unit $135.17
10. Percentage of Initial Selling Price per Unit – 13.52 %

PREPARING AND RETAINING ORDER TICKETS

Over the last few years, the necessity to maintain written memos detailing those associated with order tickets has become increasingly important. Almost all financial regulatory bodies including Financial Industry Regulatory Authority (FINRA) and National Association of Securities Dealers (NASD) have written policies related to order tickets. Specifically, the memo should detail the following:

1. The identity of the associated person responsible for the customer's account and anyone who was involved in the entering or processing of a transaction
2. Whether the order was subject to discretionary authority
3. Whether the order was accepted on a subscription basis
4. The terms and conditions of the order
5. Any modifications or cancellation of the order
6. If the order was entered into an electronic system
7. The time at which the order was executed or cancelled

ANNUAL TASKS REQUIRED BY NFA RULES

Ten annual tasks for Members required by NFA rules are:

1. Pay NFA dues
2. Complete the Annual Update/Questionnaire
3. Submit to NFA a certified annual report within the specified time
4. Complete the NFA's Self-Examination Checklist
5. Send privacy policy information to each new and existing costumer.
6. Provide ethics training to your employees and principals.
7. Conduct an audit of every Guaranteed IB and Branch office.
8. Conduct an audit of your AML program.
9. Test your Disaster Recovery Plan
10. Review Point of Contact information for USA Patriot Act 314(a)

SUBMISSION OF FINANCIAL REPORTS TO THE NFA

All financial reports are filed electronically on Form 1-FR-FCM or, for broker-dealers, the 1-FR-FCM or the FOCUS Report via the NFA's approved electronic reporting software (i.e. Winjammer). To file reports, each Member must secure from the NFA their PIN (Personal Identification Number) which is considered to be the equivalent of an authorized signature. To obtain this PIN, the Member should fill out and sign the PIN request form and submit it to the NFA. Sometimes, an NFA Member is also a member of another Commodities DSRO (Designated Self Regulatory Organization). If an NFA Member FCM is required to file(non electronically) financial reports, minimum financial requirements, or accountant qualifications with any other futures DSRO, then it must simultaneously send copies of those completed forms to the Chicago office of the NFA. If the NFA requests extra financial reports, the FCM or IB must send them promptly.

NFA's Rule 2-7

NFA's rule 2-7 (Branch office Managers and Designated Securities Futures Principals) essentially states that in order to be a Branch Manager, you have to pass the Branch Manager test. The New York Stock Exchange and Financial Industry Regulatory Authority (FINRA) also have rules that enable Associates to become Branch Managers. You could qualify for Branch manager status under their rules, but you would also need to be sponsored by a registered broker-dealer. If you pass the Branch Manager Exam-Futures, then you qualify to be a designated Securities Futures Principal for a Broker-Dealer provided you met the two other requirements: being a Member (or Associate of a Member) and being a Member's partner, officer, director, branch manager, or supervisor.

NFA Rule 2-2

The NFA's Rule 2-2 lists prohibited activities. A summary of the prohibited activities are: (see NFA rule 2-2 Fraud and related matters)

1. Members shall not cheat any commodity futures customer.
2. Member s shall not bucket commodity futures orders.
3. Members shall not willfully make false reports regarding any commodity futures contract.
4. Members shall not distribute false information that could affect the price of a commodity that is the subject of the member's commodity futures contract.
5. Members shall not manipulate the price of commodity futures contracts.
6. Members shall not willfully submit false information to the NFA.
7. Members shall not conduct trades for persons that have been prohibited from trading.
8. Members shall not steal from their customer's commodity futures trading accounts.
9. Members shall not engage in activities that require NFA registration UNLESS they are registered with NFA to do so.

Waiver of the "2 Year Continuous Experience" Rule

NFA Rule 2-8 also details the process of obtaining a waiver for the "2 year continuous experience" requirement. Normally, an AP can't have discretionary authority unless they've had at least 2 years experience. However, "equivalent experience" can be substituted for "2 years experience". It requires that the Member submit a written request to the Compliance Director, who then submits the request to a 3 member Panel for review. Members of the Business Conduct Committee and/or the Hearing Committee make up the panel and will review the request and report their decision to the Compliance Director who then informs the waiver-seeking Member. CTAs are exempt from this requirement.

Disputes Between NFA Members

Disputes between Members are generally resolved through arbitration, and attorneys may be present. Members are expected to cooperate by supplying relevant documents if requested, in a timely manner. If a Member wants to arbitrate a dispute, then a 'notice of intent to arbitrate' must be filed with the NFA secretary within two years of the offending act. The Secretary prepares a Demand for Arbitration statement and sends it to the respondent listed in the intent notice. The respondent has 45 days to answer or to submit a counterclaim.

BEHAVIORS THAT SUGGEST TERRORIST ACTIVITY

The following list of behaviors strongly indicates possible terrorist activity. A Member might be required to file a suspicious activity report if this is observed.

1. Makes large donations to unknown nonprofit organizations.
2. Conducts business with persons or organizations that are on any of the official lists of known or suspected terrorists.
3. Makes money transfers into or out of countries that the US State Department suspects of sponsoring terrorism.
4. Provides incorrect identification.
5. Uses a firm's money transfer services but rarely trades.
6. Declines to make a transaction after realizing records are kept of all such transactions.

These are just a few examples of suspicious activity.

POSITION LIMITS SET FORTH BY SECTION 150 OF THE CFTC REGULATIONS

According to Section 150 Part 2 of the Commodity Futures Trading Commission (CFTC) Regulations, no individual, association, partnership, corporation, or trust may control net long or net short commodity shares for future delivery or on a futures-equivalent basis in excess of the amounts listed on the chart below.

Speculative Position Limits by Number of Contracts

Contract	Spot Month	Single Month	All Months
Chicago Board of Trade			
Corn & Mini-Corn	600	33,000	33,000
Oats	600	2,000	2,000
Soybeans & Mini Soybeans	600	15,000	15,000
Wheat & Mini-Wheat	600	12,000	12,000
Soybean Oil	540	8,000	8,000
Soybean Meal	720	6,500	6,500
Minneapolis Grain Exchange			
Hard Red Spring Wheat	600	12,000	12,000
ICE Futures U.S.			
Cotton No. 2	300	5,000	5,000
Kansas City Board of Trade			
Hard Winter Wheat	600	12,000	12,000

INDEPENDENT AUDIT FUNCTION

All publicly traded companies have their financial statements audited. In keeping with General Accepted Accounting Principles, organizations should hire a third party certified public accountant (i.e., an independent auditor) with no known financial or personal conflicts of interest to perform the audit. Because these auditors are paid a previously negotiated rate that is not based on the opinion they issue, current and potential investors are able to feel more secure that the findings are legitimate and are in keeping with accepted industry standards.

NFA AUDIT

NFA audits are intended to accomplish the following:

- Ascertain whether the record keeping program is in compliance with the applicable rules of the NFA and the regulations of the Commodity Futures Trading Commission (CFTC).
- Ensure that the member is in compliance with NFA rules regarding sales practices (Rules 2-2, 2-4, and 2-29).

ONGOING EMPLOYEE TRAINING PROGRAM

Most anti-money laundering employee training programs can be divided into two groups: initial and ongoing. The initial training occurs when an individual is either a newly hired employee or is promoted internally. These programs provide the policies and procedures that an employee needs to be aware of to perform his or her job functions and be in keeping with all regulatory bodies as well as an introduction to any software that is used on a regular basis to detect and prevent money laundering. An ongoing employee training program, as the name would suggest, is one that takes place on a regular basis. It is especially important in industries that have regulatory and legislative rules that change or are reinterpreted on a more-than-average basis. An ongoing employee training program differs from continuing education programs in that the program is not mandated by any governmental agency but instead is sponsored by a company's Human Resources, Training, or Compliance department.

BANK SECRECY ACT ADOPTED IN 1970

The Bank Secrecy Act originally was adopted in 1970. The act was passed as a means to detect possible money laundering (from criminal activities, terrorist funding, and tax evasion). The Bank Secrecy Act (also known as the Currency and Foreign Reporting Transactions Report Act) includes requirements that have been incorporated into all financial institutions. The main requirement introduced in this legislation is the necessity to report to the Internal Revenue Service all deposits greater than $10,000. The general rule states that a business must file Form 8300 (Report of Cash Payments over $10,000 Received in a Trade or Business) if the business receives cash totaling $10,000 or more from one buyer as a result of a single or two or more related transactions. In other words, the $10,000 is a daily aggregate amount. In addition, Title III of the US Patriot Act was developed based on the Bank Secrecy Act.

OPTIONS LISTING PROCEDURE PLAN

The Options Listing Procedure Plan is an Office of the Comptroller (OCC) document that describes the procedures that listings must follow and addresses the following procedures specifically:

- Selection of an option class
- Request to review the eligibility of a new option class
- Selection of a new options series
- Permissible adjustments
- Annual notices
- How new plan sponsors may be added
- List of plan sponsors
  - BATS Exchange
  - BOX Options Exchange LLC
  - C2 Options Exchange
  - Chicago Board Options Exchange
  - International Securities Exchange
  - ISE Gemini
  - Miami International Securities Exchange
  - NASDAQ OMX BX
  - NASDAQ OMX PHLX
  - NASDAQ Stock Market
  - NYSE

CPO/CTA General

COMMODITY TRADING ADVISOR

A commodity trading advisor is an individual or an entity typically registered with and certified by the National Futures Association (NFA) that offers fee-based advice and/or analyses on commodity-based futures and/or options investing, including forward contracts and swaps.

EXEMPTION OF CPO FROM NFA REGISTRATION

A CPO may be exempt from NFA registration if certain characteristics of the pool fall below certain size and operational thresholds. For example, if a CPO's compensation is limited to cover his operating expenses, if the CPO operates only one pool, and if the pool is not advertised, then the CPO may be exempt. Another way a CPO may be exempt is if none of the pools he operates has more than 15 participants and if the total aggregate gross capital contributions for his managed pools do not exceed $400,000.

REGISTRATION REQUIREMENT EXEMPTIONS FOR CTAS

Generally speaking, an individual qualifies as a commodity trading advisor (CTA) if advice is provided either directly or indirectly. However, NFA registration rules provide a registration requirement exemption if the advice provided is not specifically tailored to the individual account of a customer. Examples would include publications such as books and periodicals, which present the same advice to all readers. Exemptions also exist for those whose advisory services are an incidental part of their trade or business. These exempt individuals include:

- individuals who advise no more than 15 people, and do not present themselves to the public as a CTA
- individuals engaged in a business subject to state regulation (such as an insurance company)
- individuals engaged in the business of cash markets, such as dealers, brokers, or sellers
- individuals engaged in various other professions specifically defined by the CEA

CTA ALSO ACTING AS IB

Generally speaking, a commodity trading advisor (CTA) also acting as an introducing broker (IB) is required to register as an IB unless one of two conditions is present:

- The accounts under management are a result of a power of attorney. OR
- Compensation is not collected on a fee per trade basis.

DISCLOSURE DOCUMENTS

The NFA Rule 2-13 CPO/CTA Regulations requires that disclosure documents include a "Break Even analysis". CFTC Regulation 4.21 requires that Disclosure Documents accurately detail all fees and expenses. It must be presented in the specific NFA format. Also, CFTC regulations 4.1, 4.7, 4.12 and 4.16 through 4.41 must be complied with. If a Member is required to file documents to CFTC under CFTC 4.7, 4.12, 4.22, 4.26 or 4.36, then copies of the documents must also be submitted to the NFA's Chicago office at the same time.

CTA

According to the CFTC a CTA, Commodities Trading Advisor, is any person who engages in the business of advising others directly, through writings, or electronic media about the value or prudence of trading in commodities. A CTA advises others for compensation or profit. The commodity contracts can be for future delivery to be made on a contract market or derivatives transaction execution facility. They can be options contracts or leverage transactions. The CTA advises, including issuing reports and analyses about commodities trading, for profit as part of a regular business. This does not include banks, trust companies, news reporters, columnist, or editors. It does not include publishers, FBs, FCMs or a fiduciary of defined benefit plans.

CPO

According to the CFTC, a CPO, a Commodity Pool Operator, is a person who engages in business that is like an investment trust or syndicate. A CPO solicits, accepts, or receives funds, securities or property from the sale of stock or securities for the purpose of trading in any commodity for future delivery or for a contract market or derivatives transaction facility. The term does not include persons who are not within the CFTC intent of the definition.

CUSTOMER INFORMATION REQUIRED TO BE RECORDED

The CFTC and the NFA require CPOs and CTAs to accurately record and maintain certain information about their customers. These records should include all of the following.

1. The name and address
2. Any Power of Attorney authorizing a discretionary account which enables the CTA to trade on their behalf.
3. Any other written agreements between the CTA and the customer
4. List of all executed transactions and confirmation of transactions
5. List of purchase and sale statements and FCM monthly statements
6. Copies of promotional materials, including date of distribution
7. Allocation information for bunched orders. CTAs provide this to the FCM

SPECIAL ACCOUNTS

Accounts that have reportable positions are considered special accounts. Exchanges, clearing agencies, FCMs and, if required by the CFTC, individual traders should submit reports about special accounts on a weekly or daily basis. A reportable position occurs when a trader acquires more contracts than are permitted without reporting them. For example, if a trader has a 100 contract reporting level, but acquires 110 contracts, then CFTC rules require that the position be reported. The contracts can be either futures or futures options. All of a trader's accounts are considered to be one account for the purpose of determining a reportable position.

FINANCIAL INFORMATION CTAS MUST PROVIDE ABOUT TRADING PROGRAMS

CTAs must provide certain financial information about the trading programs that they use for their customer's accounts. This information includes:

1. Total assets traded as of that date.
2. The largest monthly drawdown of the last five years, including year-to-date.
3. The worst peak-to-valley drawdown for the last five years including year-to-date.
4. The monthly compounded annual rates of return for the last five years including year-to-date.
5. The number of accounts that were closed in the last five years and whether they had a net profit or loss when they closed.
6. Beginning net asset value (BNAV), ending net asset value (EAV), and changes in net asset value (NAV).

Also, the statement "Past performance is not necessarily indicative of future results" should be prominently displayed along with this financial information.

HANDLING CUSTOMER DEPOSITS IN COMMODITY POOLS

Commodity pool operators (CPO) are those who handle one or more commodity pools (managed accounts or funds). Commodity pools are typically publicly offered limited partnerships, with all participants jointly liable for risk of loss. When it is a publicly offered limited partnership, the representative offering it must also be registered as a securities representative. The CPO is not the pool itself, and any customer funds deposited with the pool must be in the name of the pool, not the operator of the pool. The operator must be careful not to mingle funds from pool accounts with funds from non-pool accounts, or funds from other pools. Commodity pool operators must send annual statements for each pool they operate, to each participant of a particular pool, and to the CFTC. Account statements detailing income/loss and net asset value must be sent quarterly if the pool's net assets are less than $500,000 at the beginning of the fiscal year. If the net assets of a pool exceed $500,000, then account statements must be sent monthly.

CTA RESPONSIBILITIES REGARDING BUNCHED ORDERS

The NFA requires that CTAs be responsible for the allocation of contracts that are part of bunched orders. The CTA must confirm contract allocation on a daily basis. The CTA also is required to review their allocation program quarterly to verify that customers that are part of a particular allocating system are getting similar allocating results. Trade-by-trade allocation results are not as critical as allocation fairness over a period of time. The CTA should maintain program audit records to facilitate a thorough analysis of their program. These records should also be readily available to the NFA during an audit.

FEES OF A POOL INCLUDED IN A BREAK EVEN ANALYSIS

The NFA requires that CPOs submit a 'break even' analysis to prospective pool participants. When calculating the break even point, certain fees should be included. The fees used to calculate the break even point should be based on actual experience, if known. If actual experience information is not known, then the fees should be based on a good faith estimate (i.e. round-turn estimates previously published). Also, if the interest income generated by a pool is to be distributed to the participants, then this interest amount should be deducted from the trading expenses amount in the break even analysis. This is because this interest amount will be included as part of the return on initial investment. If any of the interest is to be paid to the pool operator, then that amount should not be deducted from trading expenses, and should be disclosed to the pool participants.

MANAGEMENT AND INCENTIVE FEES TYPICALLY CHARGED BY A CPO

The CPOs must specify each fee that is expected to be charged to a commodity pool. The fees that should be included are:

1. Management fees
2. Brokerage fees and commissions, including interest
3. Trading advice fees
4. Incentive fees
5. Any allocations to the CPO that exceed pro rata allocations
6. Solicitation commissions
7. Professional fees
8. Clearance fees paid to exchanges and SROs
9. Any other fees, commissions, expenses not listed here

CPO/CTA Disclosure Documents

DISCLOSURE STATEMENTS
CPOs

Regulation 4.24 of the Commodity Futures Trading Commission (CFTC) requires a commodity pool operator (CPO) to complete two types of disclosure statements. The two types of disclosure statements required from a CPO are as follows:

- cautionary statement – This is a statement with specific language outlined in the CFTC regulations. The statement indicates that the CFTC makes no representation about the adequacy of the disclosure.
- risk disclosure statement – This is a detailed statement with specific language outlined in the CFTC regulations. The statement concerns the inherent risks of futures transactions.

CTAs

Commodity Futures Trading Commission (CFTC) Regulation 4.35 requires two types of disclosure statements from a commodity trading advisor (CTA). The disclosure statements required from a CTA are the same ones required from a commodity pool operator. They are described below:

- cautionary statement – This is a statement with specific language outlined in the CFTC regulations. The statement indicates that the CFTC makes no representation about the adequacy of the disclosure.
- risk disclosure statement – This is a detailed statement with specific language outlined in the CFTC regulations. The statement concerns the inherent risks of futures transactions.

FIVE-YEAR BUSINESS BACKGROUND

According to Commodity Futures Trading Commission (CFTC) Regulation 4.34, any individual responsible for supervising a CTA must also provide a five-year business background. Supervisors include all individuals in the supervisory or reporting chain of command.

ALTERNATIVE TRADE

Commodity pool operators (CPOs) and/or commodity trading advisors (CTAs) are required to maintain written records on transactions that can be classified as alternative trades. Alternative trades include the following two types of transactions:

- A block trade is a single, large volume transaction that is negotiated ex-pit (outside of an exchange), and then executed on the floor of an exchange. Such transactions are subject to review and cancellation at the discretion of the Commodity Futures Trading Commission (CFTC).
- A bunched order is a single order executed on behalf of multiple customers.

56

Mometrix

PERFORMANCE INFORMATION REQUIRED BY CTAS

NFA rule 2-34 CTA performance Reporting and Disclosures describes performance information required of CTAs (Certified Trading Advisors), also when dealing with partially funded accounts. Member CTAs must calculate rate of return using nominal account size as the denominator, draw down information must also be based on rate of return using nominal account size as the denominator, and they can only use interest earned on actual funds to calculate net performance. When dealing with partially funded accounts, CTAs must provide a written confirmation that states the description of the trading program and the account size that the customer and CT have determined. New customers must receive the confirmation before the first trade. However, existing customers must be given the confirmation each time the information changes. The confirmation only needs to include new information and the effective date of the change. Additionally, CTAs must state how management fees will be computed, how the account size will be affected by cash additions and withdrawals, and a brief explanation of how partial funding affects margin, leverage, commissions, fees, and rate of return.

PERFORMANCE DISCLOSURES FOR CPOS

According to Commodity Futures Trading Commission (CFTC) Regulation 4.25.b, performance disclosure for a commodity pool operator (CPO) is required when:

- The pool has a minimum of three years of trading history.
- No less than 75% of the contributions to the pool originated from unaffiliated investors.

CFTC REGULATION 4.35

Commodity Futures Trading Commission (CFTC) Regulation 4.35 regarding financial performance records disclosure for commodity trading advisors (CTAs) requires that performance information be disclosed for the most recent five years before the current one, or for inception to present, whichever is the lesser time period. Information for the current year to date must also be provided.

INSTITUTIONAL CUSTOMERS AND INDIVIDUAL CUSTOMERS

NFA rule 2-30, Customer Info and Risk Disclosure, defines institutional customers (The NFA defines them in a double negative: "Non-institutional customers are those who do not...") Normally, Members are required to obtain personal information, like financial status, about a customer before advising them about trades in security futures products. However, the Member does not need to obtain this kind of information if the customer is an institutional customer. This includes banks, savings and loans, insurance companies, investment companies, broker-dealers, FCMs, CPOs, or CTAs. Some of these are considered 'institutional' even if they have been exempt from registration under the Commodity Exchange Act of 1940. Also, any entity that has total assets of $50million is also considered to be 'institutional', even if it is an individual.

57

Copyright © Mometrix Media. You have been licensed one copy of this document for personal use only. Any other reproduction or redistribution is strictly prohibited. All rights reserved.

CFTC REGULATION 4.24.J

Commodity Futures Trading Commission (CFTC) Regulation 4.24.j requires actual or perceived conflicts of interest on the part of certain principals of a commodity pool operator (CPO) to be disclosed. The principals that must be disclosed by the CPO include the following:

- commodity pool operators
- pool trading managers
- commodity trading advisors
- CPOs of any major investee pool
- any other persons providing services to the pool

CFTC REGULATION 4.34.J

Commodity Futures Trading Commission (CFTC) Regulation 4.34.j regarding the disclosure of perceived conflicts of interest on the part of certain principals of commodity trading advisors (CTAs) is similar to the disclosure rules for commodity pool operators (CPOs). CPOs must disclose each CTA that is advising a pool. CTAs must disclose futures commission merchants (FCMs) and introducing brokers, as well as their supervisors. In addition to CTAs, the following principals must disclose any real or perceived conflicts of interest:

- any futures commission merchant (FCM)
- any retail foreign exchange dealer (RFED)
- any introducing broker (IB)

STATEMENT OF ADDITIONAL INFORMATION

NFA Rule 2-35 'CPO/CTA disclosure documents' requires that a Statement of Additional Information(of a Disclosure Document) have a cover letter, a table of contents and the required information. The cover letter should state the name of the commodity pool, the date of the most recent Pool Disclosure Document, that it is part of the Disclosure Document, and the date of the Statement of Additional Information. The cover letter should be immediately followed by a table of contents. The Statement of Additional Information is the part that is used to expand on or explain further statements made in part 1 of the disclosure. This could be anything required by the SEC that was not included in part one. It can also list rules, statutes, or regulations for reference. It can give background information about the pool, the CPO, CTA, or other service providers. Even information about the commodity futures market or other markets that might influence this pool can be given.

NFA Rule 2-35 CPO/CTA Disclosure documents requires that the 'pool' disclosure information required by CFTC Regulations 4.21, 4.24, and, if applicable, 4.25 be included using plain language(not technical) and that any additional information be described in a "Statement of Additional Information". The pool disclosure should also describe the basic characteristics of the pool in language that is readily understandable. It should also include any information required by the Securities and Exchange Commission. If the disclosure is in several parts, it should be stated

that the document is in parts and marked accordingly (i.e. part 1of 2, part 2 of 2). This disclosure must be given prior to accepting funds from a prospective participant in the pool.

DISCIPLINARY INFORMATION INCLUDED IN DISCLOSURE DOCUMENTS

The Disclosure Document that CPOs or CTAs must provide to customers must include information about any disciplinary actions against the CPOs or CTAs. It should include any administrative, civil or criminal action that was filed within the preceding 5 years, against the CPO, pool itself, or the CTA. It should include actions against the Member as well as any pending actions. Favorable results do not need to be included. Information on the principals involved in the disciplinary action must also be listed. The principals that should be included are:

1. The CTA, CPO, and any involved IB, or FCM. 'Involved' means holding the customer's account on behalf of the CTA .
2. The pool's, trading manager, major commodity trading advisors, and major investee pool operator.

TIME LIMITATIONS OF DISCLOSURE DOCUMENTS

Disclosure Document that CTAs give to customers must include the actual performance record of all of their accounts from the last five years, including the current year. The information must be from within the last 3 months of the date of the Document. Documents that are dated more than 9 months from date of use are not permitted. If errors are found in the Disclosure Document, the CTA has 21 days to make the correction in an amendment.

INFORMATION ABOUT POOL PRINCIPALS INCLUDED IN DISCLOSURE DOCUMENTS

The Disclosure Document that a CPO/CTA must provide prospective customers must also include the business background from the last five years of pool principals. Principals can be the pool's trading manager, major investee pool operators, and major commodity trading advisors. These are persons who are officers, directors, or who influences trading decisions for the CPO. This should include:

1. The name of the principal and their employers
2. The dates of employment
3. Their business ventures and associations
4. A description of the duties they performed for each employer
5. The FCM that will execute the CPOs' trades and their IB if applicable

FEES INCLUDED IN DISCLOSURE DOCUMENTS

The Disclosure Document that a CPO/CTA must give prospective customers must also include the fees incurred or will be incurred for the operation of the pool .The following charges are examples of what kinds of fees should be included.

1. Management fees
2. Administrative fees

Mometrix

3. Trading advice fees
4. Incentives
5. Solicitation commissions
6. Commissions including interest paid to FCMs
7. Clearance fees
8. Principal protection costs
9. SRO and Exchange dues

INCLUSION OF CERTAIN TRADING RESULTS IN DISCLOSURE DOCUMENTS

The Disclosure Document required to be given to a prospective customer by a CPO/CTA must provide certain trading results, unless otherwise specified. For example, if 50% or more of the pool is owned by the CPO/CTA trading manager, affiliates or family members then the trading results are not required to be submitted. Also, if the pool is less than 3 years old and has not yet traded then trading results don't need to be disclosed. However, the CPO must prominently state "This pool has not commenced trading and has no performance history." Also, if the trading manager, pool operator, or other principal of a pool has no trading experience in any other pool, then this also must be stated prominently. "Neither this pool operator nor any of its trading principals has previously operated any other pools."

POOL PERFORMANCE INFORMATION REQUIRED IN DISCLOSURE DOCUMENTS

Disclosure Documents that a CPO/CTA must provide prospective customers must also include pool performance results. The following information must be included.

1. Date of trading commencement of the pool
2. Name of the pool
3. Type of pool
4. Aggregate gross capital subscriptions to the pool
5. The pool's current net asset value
6. Performance data from last five years from other pools of the same class, but should be less prominently displayed
7. Material differences between similar pools
8. The largest monthly drawdown and worst peak-to-valley drawdown that occurred during the last five years. This should be state as a percent of the pool's net asset value

CFTC REGULATION 4.24F

Commodity Futures Trading Commission (CFTC) Regulation 4.24.f requires a five-year business background for certain commodity pool operator (CPO) principals, including each commodity trading advisor (CTA) and investee pool operator. In addition to each CTA and investee pool operator, the CPO must disclose:

- any pool trading manager
- operators of each major investee pool
- each and every principal who participates in the decision-making process or supervises those who do

CFTC REGULATION 4.24.H

Commodity Futures Trading Commission (CFTC) Regulation 4.24.h requires disclosure of the commodity pool operator's (CPO) investment program and the use of proceeds. Such disclosure includes the types of commodities that the pool will trade and the trading and investment programs and policies that will be followed. The CPO investment program disclosure must also include the following:

- the commodity trading advisors (CTAs) that will be employed and the nature and operation of the proposed trading program
- the amount of assets that will be held in segregation in order to fulfill the margin requirements of the pool

CFTC REGULATION 4.24.I

Commodity Futures Trading Commission (CFTC) Regulation 4.24.i regarding commodity pool operators (CPOs) requires disclosure of 13 specific fees incurred by the pool. The fees that must be disclosed by a CPO include the following:

- management fees
- brokerage fees and commissions
- trading advice fees and commissions
- collective investment fees and expenses
- incentive fees
- allocations
- commissions for solicitation
- professional, general, and administrative expenses
- organizational and offering expenses
- clearance fees
- fees for principal protected pools
- bid/ask spread fees

BEHAVIOR VIOLATIONS THAT LEAD TO EXPULSION FROM THE NFA

Violations of the NFA Rule 2-30 involving risk disclosure have led to expulsion from NFA Membership. Here are some examples of the kind of activity that has resulted in expulsion:

- A factory laborer was instructed by an AP to state on his account application he was a foreman with liquid assets of $75,000 instead of $45,000.
- A customer with annual income of $24,000 was advised by an AP that his account application would be rejected if the annual income stated was not in excess of $50,000.
- An unemployed customer with no futures trading experience but who had received an inheritance of $30,000, was advised by an AP to "put down anything" on the account application for her employment and income. She received insufficient disclosure for her circumstances (she should have been told that futures trading is simply too risky for her). The AP did not explain the account documents and did not give her sufficient time to review the papers.
- A customer was advised by an AP to state he had been involved in real estate development for 18 years when he had simply owned his home for 18 years.
- A 52 year old customer with no prior trading experience was advised by an AP to indicate that his net worth was high enough to get the account approved.
- A husband and wife, with no prior trading or investment experience and insufficient funds, were advised by an AP to take out a credit card loan to meet the minimum required investment needed to open an account. They did get the loan ($3000), and added some of their own saving ($2000).The husband returned on his 30 minute lunch break to sign papers, but had no time to read them. The risk disclosure statement had not been explained to him.
- A sick 77 year old retired real estate investor and his sick wife, with limited health insurance coverage, but with a combined net worth of $100,000 and fixed annual income of $20,000, were informed by an AP that the risk of loss from futures trading was slight. The AP did not provide additional risk disclosure stating that futures trading was just too risky for them.
- An unemployed actor was instructed by an AP to state on his account application that his occupation was self-employed, and that his net worth should be high enough to get approval. Also, the AP advised that the income amount should be from before the actor became unemployed.

TYPICAL VIOLATIONS OF RECORD KEEPING AND SUPERVISING RULES

Typical violations of NFA's Compliance Rule 2-30 regarding record keeping and supervising usually involve failure to get enough customer information, like approximate age, net worth, current/annual income and previous trading experience. Also, failure to keep such records is a typical example of this violation. A Member firm is required to supervise the gathering of customer information and the submission of risk disclosure information. These violations are usually evidence of a widespread recordkeeping deficiency within a firm, but have not been the sole reason for disciplinary action.

ASSESSMENT FEE

According to NFA Bylaw 1301 (b) , a futures contract 'round-turn' includes all transactions where a futures position is closed by delivery or cash settlement, or offset by an exchange for physicals or through a transfer from one FCM to another of offsetting futures contracts. NFA assessment fees are based on a round-turn as defined here. However, an FCM is permitted to accrue a fee at any point in a round-turn, or to split a fee between transactions that would make up a round-turn. A 'per trade' is a purchase or sale (but not exercise or expiration) of an option. The NFA assessment fee will be imposed on the underlying futures transaction on a round turn basis if the option is exercised. The NFA assessment fee, payable by FCMs but invoiced to customers, is currently $.04 per round-turn. The assessment fee on options is $.02 per trade, not on per round-turn. These assessment fees also apply to 'mini contracts', and to security futures products contracts.

EXCEPTIONS

The NFA round-turn assessments are required for most futures contracts. There are some exceptions. NFA Bylaw 1301 (b) (i) states that the customer trades of Members who have "privileges of membership on a contract market where such contract is entered" are not subject to the NFA assessment fee. The NFA assessment also does not apply if the exchange formally recognizes the customer as a member and charges them exchange fees. Trades by non-US customers on foreign exchanges are not subject to the assessment fee because they are excluded from the category of 'foreign futures and options'.

Proprietary accounts can be exempt. Accounts that are wholly owned by an FCM, or belong to firms that wholly own the FCM are generally exempt from the NFA assessment fee on their trades, but only if the trades occur on an exchange where the FCM is a member. There are two exceptions. If the account is in the name of a commodity pool (not the FCM), it must pay the assessment fees. If someone other than the exempt FCM makes deposits into the account or is liable for risk of loss, then the account is subject to the assessment fee. Also, if the transaction is Over–the-Counter, and is not subject to futures exchange rules (InterContinental Exchange for example), then assessment fees do not apply.

REPORTING TO CUSTOMER

The NFA imposes assessment fees on each round-turn of a futures contract. An FCM pays the assessment but this amount cannot be combined with commissions in its statements to customers. Instead, the assessment must be shown as its own line item, or at least combined with other fee categories. If the fee amount is higher than the NFA assessment fee, this discrepancy should be explained somewhere in the statement. The commission fee should have its own line item as well. The NFA

assessment fee is invoiced to the customer in the monthly statement or in a purchase and sale statement. It can be invoiced at the opening of a futures position.

DISCLOSURE REGARDING BUNCHED ORDER ALLOCATION

In futures trading, bunched orders are when a trader places orders for multiple accounts at the same time. The allocation of the contracts to the various accounts must be fair and equitable. The CTA is responsible for allocating the contracts and is free to use any method that is fair and equitable. However, the CTA must provide the customers with information about the chosen allocation method so they can assess its fairness. The required information includes;

1. The general strategy of the CTA
2. The CTAs' inclusion of personal or other accounts in the bunched order
3. Sufficient summary data about the chosen allocation method which can then be used to compare its results with other allocation method results and other customer results

UP FRONT FEES IN DISCLOSURE DOCUMENTS

Contributions for up front fees and organizational expenses should be deducted from the initial investment and not included in the funds that are available for trading. They should be counted as a reduction in net performance. The amount should be deducted either once for the entire contribution or monthly if the contribution could be amortized. These expenses, along with the initial investment, and net proceeds available for trading, should be included on the cover page of a Disclosure Document in tabular form. If no standard units are used, then the investment unit should be $1000.00.

NFA Know Your Customer Rule

CIP

The NFA requires all Member firms to have a Customer Identification Program, or CIP. Each potential customer, whether a person or business, must submit the required information, or authorized substitution, prior to being permitted to opening an account with the firm. In addition to requiring the usual customer identification information such as name, age, address, tax id number, and business address (for non-individuals) this program should also define what types of identification documents are needed and what and when substitutes for those documents will be accepted. A government ID with photograph and/or fingerprint is the usual identification document for individuals. However, this document is usually only acceptable if submitted in person. If a Member firm uses identification information derived from or by other firms, then identification information should be gathered about that firm. All CIP information should be kept on file for a minimum of 5 years.

NFA COMPLIANCE RULE 2-30

National Futures Association (NFA) Compliance Rule 2-30 (the know your customer rule) requires that the risks of futures trading be disclosed to customers before a trading account is opened. The minimum information that must be provided by customers in order to establish a trading account is as follows:

- the name, address, and principal occupation or business of the customer
- the current estimated annual income and net worth of the customer (if the customer is an individual)
- the customer's net worth or net assets and current estimated annual income; or, if current income is not available, the customer's annual income for the previous year (if the customer is not an individual)
- the approximate age and/or date of birth of the customer (if the customer is an individual)
- an indication of the previous investment and futures trading experience of the customer
- other information considered to be reasonable and appropriate by the member or associate in order to appropriately disclose the risks of futures trading to the customer

UPDATES TO INDIVIDUAL CUSTOMER ACCOUNTS

The futures commission merchant (FCM) member who is responsible for an individual customer's account is required to contact the customer at least annually to verify that the information previously obtained from the customer is still accurate. The FCM member must also give the customer an opportunity to correct or add any necessary account information.

The responsible FCM member must determine whether an additional risk disclosure must be provided to the customer whenever he or she is notified of material changes to customer information.

CUSTOMER INFORMATION PROVIDED BY A NFA MEMBER NOT REGISTERED AS A FINRA MEMBER

When a National Futures Association (NFA) member who is not also registered as a member of the Financial Industry Regulatory Authority (FINRA) intends to trade security-based futures on behalf of a customer, information provided about the customer must include the following details:

- The intent of the customer to engage in either hedging or speculation
- The employment status of the customer (name of employer, self-employed, retired, etc.)
- The estimated net worth of the customer (cash, securities, properties, other)
- The marital status of the customer and the number of dependents
- Other information that the member or associate considers reasonable and relevant, and will allow the member or associate to provide appropriate recommendations to the customer

Disclosure by CPO and CTAs

AMENDMENTS TO THE DISCLOSURE DOCUMENT

Copies of the Disclosure Document must be submitted to the CFTC and to the NFA 21 days before it is given to a customer. If the Disclosure Document must be amended due to errors or changes, then the corrections must be made in an amendment. Corrections must be made within 21 days of discovering the need for amending. Copies of the amended portion of the document must be distributed to all involved persons, including current customers who had received the original Disclosure Document. Electronic copies are acceptable for submission to the CFTC or the NFA.

CONFLICTS OF INTEREST DISCLOSED TO A CUSTOMER

When a CTA or CPO communicates with a potential customer, a Disclosure Document must be given to the customer. This Disclosure Document must address several areas of concern. One area of concern that must be included is the CTA's or CPO's potential conflict of interest. A CPO could have conflicts of interest with the pool trading manager, a major CTA of the pool, the CPO of a major investee pool, or with any other outside party that is involved with the pool. A CTA could have conflicts of interest with the FCM or IB that would hold the customers account for the pool. Any of these relationships must be disclosed if they exist. Also, if the pool's trading program benefits the CTA or CPO, then the arrangement must be described. If the CPO, CTA, or any principal of the pool has any ownership in the pool, it must be disclosed.

Disclosure by FCM's and IB's

SUPPLEMENTAL CHECKLIST FOR FCMs

CASH FLOW AND GIVE UP TRANSACTIONS SUBSECTIONS

The Cash Flow and Give up Transactions subsections require that Member firms abide by standard procedures when dealing with cash and orders. When dealing with cash, make sure that only account owners, or authorized persons, are given cash from their account, that cash from customer is deposited promptly, and verify that wire transfers are valid prior to making the order. In trades that lack written agreements, executing brokers should first make sure that carrying brokers will accept a trade. If the executing broker notices that a customer is trading significantly different from their norm, then the behavior, along with supporting information, should be reported to the carrying broker. Carrying brokers should keep track of a customer's executing brokers and the customer's order size and position limits that are applicable to that broker.

CUSTOMER TRADING SUBSECTION

The Supplemental Checklist for FCMs –Customer Trading and Account statements requires Member firms to include all of the following on customer order tickets:

- ticket number
- date,
- commodity options/futures
- account identification
- quantity long/short
- requested price
- fill price
- put or call (options)
- strike price and premium (options)
- time stamp (options receipt and transmission, futures)

Orders that can be executed at or near the market take precedence over a firm's proprietary or other related account orders in the same commodity. So, when an executable order is received it should be immediately sent to the floor, or applicable broker, first before other proprietary orders. The fill price should be recorded and the customer notified.

Daily and monthly confirmation statements should be sent by mail or, if pre-arranged, electronically to the customer.

FINANCIAL REQUIREMENTS FOR FCMs

The CFTC requires that NFA Members registered as FCMs maintain a minimum "Adjusted Net Capital" of $1,000,000. (see CFTC regulation 1.17) FCMs that have affiliates that deal in forex (foreign exchange) transactions must maintain a minimum Adjusted Net Capital of $7,500,000. (see Bylaw 1507(b)). A forex customer's equity cannot be used as capital or counted as an asset unless it is also recorded as a matching liability. If or when an FCM's Adjusted Net Capital drops below the minimum required amount, then the FCM cannot have guaranteed IBs. If the FCM does have a guaranteed IB, then the FCM must notify the guaranteed IB, its DSRO (Designated Self Regulatory Organization) and the NFA, that it has insufficient Adjusted Net Capital. The FCM has thirty days from the issue date of this notice to meet the financial requirement. If it cannot, then it must notify the guaranteed IB, et al that the guarantee agreement will terminate in 30 days. If the FCM should meet the financial requirement prior to the termination date, it can notify the IB et al that the agreement will not terminate.

IB General

FCM AND IB

A futures commission merchant (FCM), also known as a commission house or carrying firm, is an individual or organization that is actively engaged in the process of soliciting and accepting orders for futures and options contracts and executing such orders through an exchange. In addition, an FCM maintains an accounting system to establish individual customer accounts and accept payments for orders. An introducing broker (IB) is an individual or an organization that performs the same customer-facing activities as an FCM, but neither accepts nor accounts for customer payments. Therefore, an IB is required to maintain an affiliation or other relationship with an FCM, which will manage customer accounting and payment receipt. If an FCM agrees to act as a guarantor for the activities of an IB, the guarantor FCM must administer the customer accounting and payment receipts. Otherwise, an IB can use the services of any qualified FCM.

PROCESSING CUSTOMER TRANSACTIONS

An IB cannot accept customer funds, and therefore requires the services of an FCM. The FCM may act either in a service provider capacity, where the IB remains independent, or in a guarantor capacity. An IB acting under a guaranty agreement with an FCM is required to process all customer activity through the guarantor FCM. An independent IB is not restricted to using a specific FCM to process customer account activity.

FCM, IB, FT, AND FB

FCM, IB, FT, and FB are:

- FB- Floor Broker is a person who buys or sells commodities *for other's accounts,* for future delivery, in a place provided by a contract market or derivatives transaction execution facility.
- FT-A Floor Trader is a person who buys or sells commodity's *for their own account,* for future delivery, in a place provided by a contract market or derivatives transaction execution facility.
- FCM- A Futures Commission Merchant is a party who solicits or accepts orders to buy or sell commodities, not necessarily in a place provided by a contract market et al, but still subject to the rules set by the contract market. An FCM *does* accept money, or equivalent, for margin to secure the trades.
- IB-An Introducing Broker is a person who solicits or accepts orders for commodities, for future delivery, not necessarily in a place provided by the contract market et al, for future delivery, who *does not* accept money, or equivalent, for margin to secure accounts. An IB must be sponsored by an FCM.

70

ACCEPTING CUSTOMER DEPOSITS

Although IBs are not permitted to accept money or its equivalent from customers for trades, they are permitted to accept money or its equivalent if it is in the carrying FCM's name. The FCM must have full disclosure of all the IBs' customer accounts, including all option customers, and keep these records maintained. The FCM must execute the trades promptly upon receipt. IBs cannot have omnibus or proprietary accounts, and cannot secure or guarantee customer trades. Also, any APs (registered Associated Person) of the IB must have written permission from their IB to have an account with the carrying FCM. Written records and statements for such an account must be sent to the IB regularly.

An IB is required to use the services of an associated futures commission merchant (FCM) for receipt of all customer funds, including securities and property. The sole exception is receiving checks from a customer that are made payable to an FCM. In this situation, the IB must be acting as a conduit for bank deposit or delivery. Regulations prevent an IB from accepting customer funds with the exception of checks made payable to a futures commission merchant (FCM). Therefore, an IB must register as an FCM in order to accept customer payments. An IB that registers as an FCM is subject to a higher threshold with respect to minimum capital and reporting requirements.

GUARANTEED IB AND NON-GUARANTEED IB

An Introducing Broker (IB) solicits or accepts orders for futures contracts, but does not accept money for the orders. Instead, the funds are accepted in the name of the FCM who sponsored the IB. That sponsoring FCM clears the trades for the IB. There are basically two kinds of IBs. One is a 'guaranteed IB' and one is a 'non-guaranteed IB'. Both must arrange to have an FCM through which they clear their trades. An FCM who has a guarantee agreement with an IB becomes liable for the actions of that IB, and jointly subject to disciplinary action by the NFA. The non-guaranteed IB is solely responsible for their own actions regarding compliance with NFA rules.

FCM THAT GUARANTEES AN IB
MINIMUM CAPITAL REQUIREMENT

A futures commission merchant (FCM) that wishes to affiliate with an introducing broker via a guaranty agreement is subject to additional minimum capital requirements. The minimum capital requirements for an FCM that guarantees an IB are as follows:

- 150% of the capital required for a non-guaranty FCM
- if less than $2 million, $9,000 for each remote location operated, including each guaranteed IB
- if less than $2 million, $4,500 for each sponsored AP, including each guaranteed AP

- for securities dealers, the amount required by the SEC
- 110% of the following calculated value: 8% of the total risk margin for all customer account positions plus 8% of the total risk margin for all FCM proprietary positions

RESPONSIBILITIES

Any FCM that enters into a guaranty agreement with an IB using the required guaranty form guarantees the performance of the IB, and shall be jointly and severally liable for all obligations of the IB under the Commodity Exchange Act (CEA). In addition, National Futures Association (NFA) Compliance Rule 2-23 states that a guarantor FCM assumes responsibility for acts and omissions of the member IB that are in violation of NFA requirements and occur during the term of the guaranty agreement. In this situation, the guarantor FCM is subject to the same disciplinary action as the IB.

MINIMUM CAPITAL LEVELS FOR AN INDEPENDENT INTRODUCING BROKER AND A GUARANTEED IB

An independent IB is required to maintain adjusted net capital in the amount of the greater of:

- $45,000
- if less than $1 million, $6,000 for each remote operation
- if less than $1 million, $3,000 for each sponsored associated person

The capital requirements for a guaranteed IB are included as part of the guarantor futures commission merchant (FCM) requirements.

CAPITAL REQUIREMENTS FOR AN FCM

A futures commission merchant (FCM) is required to maintain adjusted net capital in the amount of the greater of:

- $1 million
- if less than $2 million, $6,000 for each remote operation (including IBs)
- if less than $2 million, $3,000 for each sponsored associated person (AP), including any AP of an IB
- 8% of the total risk margin for all customer account positions, plus 8% of the total risk margin for all FCM proprietary positions

SUPPLEMENTAL CHECKLIST FOR FCMS

FINANCIALS SUBSECTION

Supplemental Checklist for FCMs-Financial requires that a Member firm regularly maintain their financial records and submit required statements by their deadlines. Specifically, all accounts must be balanced and reconciled, a general ledger must be reviewed and maintained, and records, both financial and compliance, must be secured for 5 years.

Firms must appoint some qualified person to approve journal entries, and some qualified person(s) to prepare financial statements and keep track of the firm's adherence to 'minimum capital requirements' for trading. Only authorized persons should have access to accounting records. Customer accounts should be clearly designated and kept separate from the Member firm's accounts. Daily segregation, secured amount, and monthly capital computations must be made and recorded by their respective ongoing deadlines.

Due Diligence Subsection

The Supplemental Checklist for FCMs- Due Diligence Prior to Trading requires Member firms to help the customer make informed, efficient, and confidential decisions about their trading. Customer characteristics should be assessed and used to create trading guidelines for each customer prior to permitting the customer to trade. Customer trading information should not be used in any way to benefit other customers. The firm should clearly explain the variety of risks involved in trading and take measures to protect the privacy of customer information. Risks related to trading or clearing on different firms or exchanges should be thoroughly described. Since different accounts might have different goals, a firm should define the trading goals of a particular account, and not deviate from those goals. Independent account managers and employee managers should not deviate from the goals of their particular account.

AML Subsection

The Supplemental Checklist for FCMs –AML (Anti-Money Laundering plan) requires Member firms to train employees to recognize and report unusual trading activity. Examples of such activities ("red flags") include unexpected or excessive money transfers, especially when transfers are made to high risk countries or organizations. The employee should know that suspicious activity should be reported to their supervisor, especially if it might violate the BSA (Bank Secrecy Act) regarding funds transfer. The supervisor, who should be very familiar with the BSA, will determine whether a "Suspicious Activity Report" should be filed with FinCen (Financial Crimes Enforcement Network). High level political persons should have their accounts reviewed closely. Audits of the firm's AML program should be conducted annually. This should include testing by a qualified outside party. Results of the audit should be reviewed by the management, and any problem areas should be corrected.

Expectations When FCMs and IBs Handle Futures Option Contracts

The NFA requires that all FCMs and IBs that deal with futures options contracts must have written procedures for executing these transactions. Each option customer's account must be adequately supervised. This includes any account solicitations and customer complaints. The procedures should address the fair allocation of exercise notices. The solicitation and sale of deep out-of-the-money options should also be closely monitored. An explanation of the different terms used in futures options trading should also be included, as needed, to prospective customers.

EXTRA INFORMATION REQUIRED WHEN TRADING ON FOREIGN EXCHANGES

If an FCM or IB plans to trade on foreign exchanges then additional risk disclosure documents are required. The customer agreement could contain the written authorization to trade on foreign exchanges. If it does not, then the authorization must be in a separate Risk Disclosure Document. In either case, the risk disclosure should explain some key points.

1. Trading on foreign exchanges does not have the same protections that are granted to trading on domestic exchanges.
2. Foreign futures transactions are cleared on foreign exchanges.
3. There is no domestic organization that regulates foreign exchanges.
4. There is no domestic organization that enforces the laws of the foreign country that hosts the foreign exchange.
5. Fluctuations in foreign exchange rates might have an added affect on the profit or loss realized when trading on foreign exchanges.

INFORMATION REQUIRED BEFORE HIRING NEW PERSONNEL

When a Member firm hires new personnel it is very important that adequate information be obtained about the potential employee as well as about their former employers. This is to help determine if the candidate is qualified and how much supervision will be required to comply with NFA regulations. Specifically, any 'yes' answers on Form 8-R should investigated by reviewing the supporting documents of Form 8-R. NFA records about the candidate should be obtained and derogatory or possibly disqualifying information should be noted. Previous employers should be questioned about the candidate's performance. Also, the previous employer's record should be reviewed for futures-related disciplinary actions, as this information could involve the prospective employee.

BUNCHED ORDERS

FRAUDULENT ALLOCATION

The NFA requires that if/when the FCM observes any fraudulent contract allocations of bunched orders, it must take appropriate measures to inform the regulatory agencies of the improper allocation. If an FCM executes and clears bunched orders, it is in a better position to be aware of improper allocations. However, it is uncommon that an FCM has sufficient information to determine if there is fraudulent allocation. Still, if the FCM does have reason to believe the allocation is unfair, then the FCM must make an inquiry about the allocation and then, if needed, refer the matter to the CFTC, NFA or other DSRO.

RESPONSIBILITIES

The CFTC requires that the CTA be responsible for developing a contract allocation plan for bunched orders. However, the FCM is obligated to obtain sufficient information from the account manager to follow the instructions. In a 'give-up' arrangement, the executing FCM must obtain information about the account manager at the time of order placement and instructions for the contracts to 'give up' to each clearing FCM. The clearing FCM must receive information about the number of contracts to be allocated to each account in the bunched order, as well as how to allocate split and partial fills among accounts. Even though NFA rules state that the CTA is responsible for allocating contracts to bunched orders, it does not prohibit FCMs from assuming allocation responsibilities. However, the NFA requires documentation of bunched order agreements. Any allocation agreements between the CTA and an FCM must be documented. Any instructions by the CTA regarding allocation should be written and submitted to the FCM prior to, or at the time of, executing the orders. After the orders are executed, the FCM should verify that the trades cleared correctly with the correct account receiving the right allocation.

POPULARITY

Bunched orders are increasingly popular because of the increased use of electronic ordering systems. Orders can be allocated accurately and executed efficiently due to sophisticated computer programs. Managed funds and frequent 'give ups' also make bunched order a natural choice for trading contracts. Bunched orders also make the trading of hundreds of accounts in worldwide markets convenient and accurate. Consequently, their use is increasing the incidence of 'give ups', when one FCM executes a trade and a different FCM clears the trade. However, it should be noted that some allocation methods are more suitable for some CTAs due to their high volume of daily bunched order trades. Other CTAs, who trade less frequently, would likely not find bunched orders efficient or appropriate.

ALLOCATION METHODS

In futures trading, bunched orders are a group of orders for multiple accounts placed by the trader at the same time. The allocation of the contracts to the various accounts must be fair and equitable. The CTA is responsible for allocating the contracts and is free to use any method that is fair and equitable. There are several acceptable allocation methods. One example of an acceptable method is Rotation of Accounts. This involves a rotation of the accounts that receive the most favorable fills, on a daily or weekly regular cycle.

For example, if a CTA has 100 accounts as part of a bunched order program, then the fill orders would go like this:

> Cycle 1- best fill-account # 1
> 2nd best fill-account #2
> 3rd best fill- account #3
> Etc.
> The least favorable fill –account
> #100
> Cycle 2- best fill- account #2
> 2nd best fill- account #3
> 3rd best fill- account #4
> Etc.
> The least favorable fill- account #1

75

Average Price method: Because bunched orders involve large numbers of trade orders, it is often difficult to fill an order at the instructed price. The CTA must decide what allocation method to use when filling orders. With other allocation methods, some orders are filled at the best price, some at a less favorable price. The Average Price method attempts to avoid that preferential treatment of orders. Instead, a computer program is used to automatically calculate the average price for a bunched order. Then the program assigns that average price to every allocated contract. The program could also allocate the various actual fill prices to the accounts to get as close to the average fill price as possible.

NFA RECORDKEEPING RULE 2-10 FOR FCMS AND IBS

Both FCMs and independent IBs are subject to minimum capital requirements and, as such, are subject to the financial reporting requirements listed below. These requirements are above and beyond those that are applicable to all NFA members.

- Financial reports required to be filed with the Commodity Futures Trading Commission (CFTC) and/or the NFA must be prepared in English, must use U.S. dollars, and must comply with U.S. accounting standards.
- A general ledger must be maintained in English, and must use U.S. dollars.

REQUIREMENTS FOR MARGINS EXPRESSED IN FOREIGN CURRENCIES

Initial and maintenance margin deposit levels required of customers of both futures commodity merchants (FCMs) and introducing brokers (IBs) are determined by the exchange, and are usually expressed in U.S. dollars. An FCM or an IB may accept foreign currency margin deposits if a subordination agreement is in place with the owner of the account and the FCM or IB ascertains that the rules of the exchange allow the use of such instruments.

General Account Handling and Exchange Regulations

ORDER TYPES

The National Futures Association recognizes five basic types of orders common to most exchanges:

- market order
- limit order
- stop order
- stop limit order
- market if touched (MIT) order

The following is a schematic of the five basic order types:

FIVE BASIC ORDER TYPES

lower price		market price		upper price
	best price to sell	LIMIT ORDER	best price to buy	
sell at market		STOP ORDER		buy at market
	best price to sell	STOP-LIMIT ORDER	best price to buy	
buy below market		MARKET-IF-TOUCHED ORDER		sell above market
		MARKET ORDER		
		buy or sell at market		

MARKET ORDERS

Investors who trade securities on the secondary market must purchase stocks and bonds from other investors rather than from the issuer. Investors can make several types of orders relating to their securities purchase. A market order is a type of order that requires the investor's order to be carried out as soon as the investor makes the order. An investor who submits a market order will have the order carried out immediately at whatever price exists when the order is executed despite the price that existed when the order was submitted. A market order guarantees that the order will be executed. It does not guarantee the price at which the order will be executed.

MARKET ORDERS AND STOP ORDERS

If a market order is placed, the intent of the trader is to execute the order immediately at the best possible price. A floor broker will fill the order based upon the prevailing offer, bid, or ask. When a stop order is placed, the order is not executed until either a lower or upper trigger price is reached. At that point, the order is executed at the next market price.

MARKET ORDER & STOP ORDER

BUY LIMIT AND SELL LIMIT ORDERS

Investors who trade securities on the secondary market must purchase stocks and bonds from other investors rather than from the issuer. Investors can make several types of orders relating to their securities purchase. A limit order sets a minimum or maximum price at which an investor wants an order executed. An investor will place a buy limit order when they want to set a maximum price to pay for a security. The buy limit order will only be executed if the price is at or below the maximum limit. If the price exceeds this limit the order will not be executed. An investor places a sell limit order when they want to set a minimum price that they will accept for a security. Like the buy limit order, the sell limit order is not guaranteed to be executed. It will only be executed at or above the specified minimum price.

BUY STOP, SELL STOP, AND STOP LIMIT ORDERS

Buy stop, sell stop and stop limit orders are all types of stop orders. A stop order requires that the investor set a stop price or trigger price. Once a stock price reaches or passes the trigger price a stop order becomes a market order. The stop price in a buy stop order is set above a security's current price. When the price reaches or exceeds the stop price, the securities can are purchased by the investor. The stop price in a sell stop order is set below the current market price of the security. If the price reaches or drops below the stop price, the securities are sold by the investor. Stop limit orders combine the features of stop orders and limit orders. Investors who issue a stop limit order set two prices: a stop price and a limit price. The order is executed once the price reaches the stop price but it cannot be executed if the price goes beyond the limit price set by the investor.

AT-THE-OPENING AND GOOD-TILL-CANCELED

An at-the-opening order type is one that will be executed at the opening bell of the stock exchange. This order can be entered as a market order (meaning the trade will take place regardless of the price) or can be entered with a limit or stop price attached to it so that the transaction will occur only if the opening price is above (if selling) or below (if buying) a certain threshold. A good-till-canceled order is one that will stay on the books of the broker-dealer until it can be executed unless the customer chooses to cancel it before it is executed. This is helpful if the customer knows he or she wants to execute a trade once a certain threshold is met but does not know when or if that price will be met.

STOP ORDERS AND STOP LOSS ORDERS

These types of orders are used by customers who wish to avoid an excessive loss. Stop orders are also called stop loss orders. Stop orders require the investor to set a stop price. The stop order only becomes executable once the stock price has gone through the stop price. The stop price acts as a trigger—once a stock price reaches the stop price, the stop order is executed. Stop orders can be buy stop orders or sell stop orders. When a stock's price passes through the trigger price, the order is executed according to the customer's directions. Setting a stop price allows the customer to exercise a higher degree of control on a trade. The customer can set the stop price at the level they feel would most benefit their needs.

CONVERSION OF STOP ORDER TO MARKET ORDER

A stop order is a market order that becomes effective only after a certain trigger price is reached. In effect, a stop order converts to a market order at the trigger price, and the transaction is executed at the next market price. A sale stop order is priced lower than the present market to avoid losses due to continuing price declines. Conversely, a buy stop order is priced above market to avoid continuing price increases.

MARKET ORDER & STOP ORDER

RELATION OF LIMIT ORDER TO STOP LIMIT ORDER

A limit order is, in effect, a market order with upper and lower price parameters. The order establishes a floor or ceiling on the price at which the trade can be executed. The floor trader is expected to achieve either the limit price or better (OB). A stop limit order combines the characteristics of a trigger price (as in a stop order) and a floor or ceiling price (as in a limit order). Once the market price

reaches the trigger price, the trader is instructed to buy or sell at the next most favorable price above the floor or below the ceiling.

LIMIT ORDER & STOP ORDER

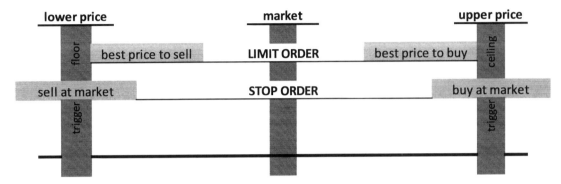

Not Held, Market on Open, and Market on Close Orders

When an investor has faith in the abilities of their broker or trader, they can issue not held orders. Not held orders, called NH orders, allow the broker to determine the best time and price at which to execute the order. Not held orders are guaranteed to be executed but the investor has no control over the price at which execution will occur. Market on open (MOO) and market on close (MOC) orders are executed at the current price when the market opens or closes. The orders can be partially executed but any portion that is not filled is cancelled. Both MOC and MOO orders must be submitted by a certain time in order to be accepted. Once submitted, MOO and MOC orders cannot be modified. Cancellations are accepted only if they are submitted by a certain time.

All or None, Immediate or Cancel, and Fill or Kill

There are several types of market orders that investors may enter. An all or none order, called AON orders, requires that an entire lot of securities must be sold or none of them can be sold. Partial execution is not possible for this type of order. Immediate or cancel orders, IOCs, require that the buy or sell order take place as soon as the investor gives the order. Any part of the order that is not immediately filled is cancelled. Partial execution is an option in IOC orders. Fill or kill, or FOK, orders do not allow partial execution. Like AON orders, FOK orders require the order to be filled in its entirety or it is completely cancelled. While AON orders can be executed over an extended amount of time, FOK orders must be executed immediately after the investor gives the order.

Updates to Individual Customer Account Information

The futures commission merchant (FCM) member who is responsible for an individual customer's account is required to contact the customer at least annually to verify that the information previously obtained from the customer is still accurate. The FCM member must also give the customer an opportunity to correct or add any necessary account information.

The responsible FCM member must determine whether an additional risk disclosure must be provided to the customer whenever he or she is notified of material changes to customer information.

USE OF MARGINS TO PROVIDES LEVERAGE

In order to establish a trading account, an individual is required to deposit sufficient funds with an exchange to satisfy both the initial and ongoing (maintenance) margin requirements, which are defined by the exchange. The amount of margin is adjusted periodically based on the volatility of the underlying commodity, but is always a fraction of the value of a contract. Consider the recent information from the New York Mercantile Exchange (NYMEX) for March sweet light crude oil futures:

- Price: $93.51 per barrel
- Contract Size: 1,000 barrels
- Maintenance Margin Requirements: $4,850 per contract

At current prices, a single contract has a value of $93,510. As a result (and assuming the margin reflects the most recent adjustments by the exchange), a trader can buy or sell a contract that is leveraged at roughly 19 times the investment, a margin requirement of about 5%. In contrast, the margin requirements for an equity trading account are often 50% or more.

FUTURES TRADERS

Margin requirements on futures exchanges are significantly lower than those required for equity trading, usually in the range of 5-20% per contract (depending upon the commodity and the exchange), as opposed to 50% or more for equities. Futures traders can therefore control contracts that are worth as much as 20 times the value of the initial margin investment. For speculators, margins create opportunities for large dollar gains, even when changes in prices are relatively small. In the case of hedging, margins can provide significant amounts of risk exposure at a reasonable cost.

VARIATION CALL

A variation call is issued by a clearinghouse to a member when the net position value of the member and, separately, each customer of the member, falls below the maintenance margin requirements. The subsequent payment to restore the maintenance margin is the variation margin amount. For example, consider the recent information from the New York Mercantile Exchange (NYMEX) for March sweet light crude oil futures:

- Price: $93.51 per barrel
- Contract Size: 1,000 barrels
- Maintenance Margin Requirements: $4,850 per contract

Assuming the margin amount above reflects the latest adjustments by the exchange and the trader holds one contract, a $1 decline in the price per barrel would create a $1,000 loss to the trader, which is charged to the trader's account. If the subsequent

value of the account falls below $4,850, a variation call would be issued to the trader in the amount required to restore the value of the account to the maintenance margin amount.

MARGIN REQUIREMENTS FOR FUTURES TRADERS

Margin requirements are established by each individual exchange, and they vary based upon the underlying commodity supporting the contract. Brokers may require higher margins of their customers than those set by an exchange, but these margins can never be lower than the ones set by an exchange. Various statistical analyses are used by exchanges to measure price volatility and set margin requirements accordingly. The amount of margin required is set at a per contract level. At this set level, traders can be expected to cover any probable losses in the case of normal price fluctuations. For example, margins on the Chicago Mercantile Exchange (CME) are expected to be sufficient to cover as much as 99% of the probable price changes during a given trading day or multiple trading days. Changes in the underlying factors that can cause price volatility (supply disruptions, conflicts, disasters, government policy, etc.) are monitored, and margin levels are adjusted as volatility is affected.

INITIAL MARGINS AND MAINTENANCE MARGINS AND EFFECTS OF MARGIN CALLS

The amount of initial margin is that which is required to open a trading account and establish a market position. Thereafter, if a trader experiences adverse changes that reduce the account value below a certain level, additional funding (often called a margin call) is required. This maintenance margin amount is the minimum that must remain on deposit over the life of the account, and is analogous to a minimum balance required for a bank account.

For example, the recent margin levels required to trade cocoa and coffee on the NYMEX were set as indicated below:

Product	Start Period	End Period	Initial	Maintenance.
NYMEX COCOA	Mar-15	Dec-16	1,870 USD	1,700 USD
NYMEX COFFEE	Mar-15	Dec-16	4,950 USD	4,500 USD

REQUIRED DOCUMENTATION REGARDING TERMS AND CONDITIONS OF MARGINS

Brokers are required to maintain documentation regarding the terms and conditions of margins. These so-called margin agreements specify the procedures that customers are required to follow to respond to margin requirements. For example, a brokerage may require customers to respond to margin deficiencies the same day such deficiencies are incurred. Other brokers may allow customers to respond to margin deficiencies the following day. Some brokers may accept a check as payment, while others may require payment by wire transfer that is supported by a wire transfer agreement.

SETTING INITIAL AND MAINTENANCE MARGIN REQUIREMENTS

Margin requirements set by an exchange are a function of the price volatility of the underlying commodity, not only current and historic volatility, but also volatility that is expected in the future. For example, the Chicago Mercantile Exchange (CME) sets maintenance margins at a level sufficient to provide funding for 99% of the probable price change in a commodity during a given day or over a series of days. Initial margins are a function of maintenance margins, and are usually a certain percentage higher than maintenance margins (though this relationship can also be reversed). For example, recent maintenance margins at the CME for EUR/USD contracts were set at $2,500. The initial margin was 10% higher at $2,750. Margins may also be set at different levels depending upon the trading strategy. For example, speculative account margins are set at a higher level than the margins for hedging accounts.

EFFECTS ON MARGIN REQUIREMENTS WHEN AN OPTION WITH AN UNDERLYING FUTURES CONTRACT IS EXERCISED

The exercise of this type of option results in the receipt of a long or short futures position based on the type of option (put or call, long or short). The receipt of the futures contract necessitates an immediate mark to market based on the current futures price and the option strike price. If the futures position is not immediately liquidated (closed out), it becomes a new position, necessitating the posting of an initial margin per the rules of the exchange.

MARGIN REQUIREMENTS FOR A SPREAD TRADER WHO HEDGES AND A SPREAD TRADER WHO SPECULATES

Margins are known as performance bonds, and this term reflects their essential purpose. They are a risk management tool intended to guarantee contract performance in the event that adverse circumstances arise. Since hedgers maintain an underlying cash position, they have a greater ability to meet their obligations than speculators, whose cash positions are said to be "naked." Spread margins are calculated using individual outright margins as a basis. These margins are adjusted to reflect the reduced risk of an order with offsetting (short and long) positions. Since outright margins are higher for speculators than they are for hedgers, the resulting spread margins are higher as well.

The following is a simple example:

SOYBEAN MEAL CALENDAR SPREAD	Outright Margin	Contract Ratio	Total Margin	Spread Credit	Spread Margin
1 LONG SOYBEAN MEAL	$ 2,000	1	$ 2,000	87.5%	$ 250
1 SHORT SOYBEAN MEAL	$ 2,000	1	$ 2,000	87.5%	$ 250
			$ 4,000		$ 500

TRANSFER OF ACCOUNT FROM ONE MEMBER TO ANOTHER

Rule 2-7 describes what is required when customer accounts are transferred from one Member to another. When a customer want to transfer account or parts of their account to another NFA Member then the customer must submit to the carrying Member written and signed instructions. These instructions should include the customer's name, address, account number, and which parts or all of the account should be transferred. The carrying broker must then verify that the receiving Member is willing to accept the account. If so, then the carrying Member must report to the receiving Member, within 2 business days, all balances in the account. In addition to money, the 'balances' could be securities, open positions, or other property. Within 3 business days of this reporting, the carrying Member must transfer the balances to the receiving Member. These rules do not prohibit oral transfer requests by the customer.

FOREX

According to NFA Bylaw 1507 Definitions- forex, the term "forex" means foreign currency futures and options and any other contract or transaction in foreign currency that is offered on a leveraged or margined basis. It can be financed by the party offering the contract, the counterparty, or any person acting with either of these. It can also refer to contracts offered or entered into with parties not eligible to trade in the US. It can also refer to contracts not subject to rules of a contract market, a national securities exchange, a derivatives execution facility or a foreign board of trade. The term does not "include any security that is not a security futures product, any contract of sale that results in actual delivery within two days, or any contract of sale that creates an enforceable obligation to deliver between a seller and buyer that have the ability to deliver and accept delivery, respectively, in connection with their line of business, unless the transaction involves a futures contract or an option." Such contracts are considered subject to NFA regulation and oversight.

FUTURES

According to NFA Bylaw 1507 Definitions, the definition of 'futures' is defined as an option contract granted by a registered person who is qualified to grant such option contract under Commission rules. This includes foreign futures and foreign options transactions. It also includes leverage transactions and security futures products. It includes contracts on commodities such as corn, soybean oil, metals, and financial products.

NFA ANNUAL DUES REQUIREMENTS

NFA Bylaw 1301 states that annual dues should be paid in advance on January 1st of each year. Late payments cause Members to be subject to late payment fines of a certain amount per month (currently $25).Assessments based on transactions will be paid 30 days of the end of each month. Late assessment payments are subject to interest charges (set by the President and Executive committee, currently 10%) on the unpaid portions for every month the payment is late. If the Member calculates an overpayment, then they may request a ref und within 18 months of the payment due date. After that time, no refunds will be given.

ASSESSMENT CONTRACT MARKET MEMBER MUST PAY

Contract market Members must pay an assessment based on each round-turn transaction to the NFA. The assessment will not exceed a set amount (currently $150,000) for Members whose transaction volume (the number of commodity futures contracts entered into) was more than 20% of aggregate contract market transaction volume (the total number of contracts entered into on all U.S. contract markets).For those with less than 20%, the assessment will not exceed a lesser amount (currently $100, 000). The number of contracts can be adjusted due to differences in contract size. For example, one 5000 bu contract would equal five 1000bu contracts of the same commodity.

ASPECTS OF COMMODITY POOLS

The Principal who supervises trading decisions of the pool is the Trading Principal. The Trading Manager is the person authorized to allocate pool assets to CTAs or investee pools. The Trading manager is not the CPO of that pool. A multi- advisor pool is one in which the CTAs are allocated less than 25% of the pool's funds, and the investee pools have less than 25% of the pool's net asset value. A Principal-protected pool or Guaranteed Pool "limits the loss of the initial investment of its participants". The amount of losses a Pool (or account) suffers over a given period of time is called the 'draw-down'. For example, 'a draw down of 5 to 9- 96/15%' means the draw down period that lasted from May to September of 1996 had a loss of 15%. The break even point must be calculated and disclosed to pool participants. It is the profit required in the first year to equal all investment fees and expenses. It should be shown as a percentage of the initial investment, and as an actual dollar amount.

SFPs

According to the CFTC, SFPs (Security Futures Products) are sales contracts for future delivery of a single stock or a narrow based security index. It includes any put, call, straddle, or option on a security future. The security must be common stocks and must be registered with the SEC (Securities Exchange Commission). The security could also be ADRs (American Depository Receipts), ETFs (Exchange Traded Funds), TIRs (Trust Issued Receipts) or Close-End fund shares. Narrow-based security is an index with 9 or fewer main securities which are weighted according to CFTC requirements. SFPs can be traded on any CFTC designated facility, provided that facility met all the CFTC requirements, and is also registered with the SEC.

FORWARD CONTRACT AND FUTURES CONTRACT

Two general categories of contracts exist in futures trading. They are forward (or cash) contract, and futures contracts. Both are legally binding agreements to buy or sell some commodity or financial instrument in the future. However, forward contracts are not standardized. They are privately negotiated contracts between buyer and seller. Futures contracts are standardized in terms of quality, quantity, delivery time, and location. Futures contracts have the obvious benefit in that they are more liquid because they are standardized. Liquidity of a commodity is a characteristic that allows large transactions to occur without a significant impact on the price of that commodity. This is possible due to the high quantity of units of the particular commodity. Institutional traders prefer liquid investments to help minimize market fluctuations due to their own trading activities.

HEDGING

Hedging is when someone seeks to minimize their risk by offsetting their sale or purchase with an equal but opposite sale or purchase. The futures market enables efficient hedging because of the sheer volume and uniformity of contracts available to all traders. Hedgers produce or need the commodity (i.e. farmers or food processors).They want to lock in prices today for their future needs, so they can plan their budgets and estimate their profits.

Specifically, a hedger will sell a certain amount of futures contracts today to protect against a possible lower price in the future. If prices are lower in the future, then the hedger will buy an equal amount of contracts at that future time, thus realizing a profit (or at least not suffering a loss).This is called selling short or a selling hedge. Buying long, or a buying hedge, is the opposite. The Hedger buys a certain amount of contracts today. If the future price is higher, then they will sell an equal amount of futures contracts at that future time.

ORIGINAL MARGIN, CLEARING MARGIN, AND MARGIN CALL

The original margin (or initial margin) is the amount a market participant is required to deposit (a security deposit) into his margin account with a broker before any orders are placed to buy or sell futures or options contracts. The amount of funds required is determined by the contract value and market risk (Performance Bond Margin). The customer margin funds are monitored by FCMs and can vary as the market changes. Though there is a set minimum amount a customer must maintain in their account. This money serves as a guarantee that sellers and buyers can fulfill their contract obligations. Margin funds are required of individual account holders (customer margin) as well as corporate account holders (clearing margin). Clearing Margins are usually greater than customer margins, to ensure that they can fulfill their customer's contracts. A margin call is a notice to deposit more funds into margin account to meet minimum requirements. A clearing house notifies its clearing members, and a brokerage firm notifies its customers.

'IN-THE-MONEY' OPTION

When an option has a strike price that is equal or almost equal to the current market price of the underlying futures contract then it is an 'at-the-money' option. If a *call* option has a strike price that is *below* the current futures contract price, it is 'in-the-money'. If a *put* option has a strike price that is *above* the futures contract price it is also 'in-the-money'. They still have intrinsic value. If a call option strike price is above, or a put option strike price is below, the current futures contract price, then it has no intrinsic value. This has become an 'out-of –the-money' option. Intrinsic value is the amount an option is still 'in-the-money'.

OPTION ON A FUTURES CONTRACT

An option is an agreement that grants the right, but not the obligation, to purchase or sell a specific futures contract, at a specific time for a specific price. The option buyer (or option holder) pays a premium to the option seller for the right to buy the contract. The option seller (or writer) receives the premium when the holder exercises their right.   A call option is the right to buy (go long) the particular futures contract at a specific price (the strike price) before expiration of the futures contract. A put option is the right to sell (go short) a particular contract at a specific price (strike price). To assign the contract means that the option buyer is obligated to assume the underlying short or long futures position indicated in the original option.

LIMITS SET BY THE CFTC

To ensure market stability the CFTC sets limits, or trading limits, on the number of speculative futures contracts someone can hold. The CFTC also will set limits on the advance or decline from the previous day's settlement. This is also to maintain stability, by preventing major market disruptions that can have devastating economic effects.

The Chicago Board of Trade (CBOT) also sets expandable allowable price ranges during periods of volatile markets, also to maintain market stability.

REGULATION OF BUNCHED ORDERS

The NFA describes bunched orders as large order executions that facilitates the simultaneous buy and sell orders of different principals. This can be done through electronic trading. The NFA requires that the allocation of these multiple accounts be regulated, that is, the individual orders should be filled with specific allocating procedures to ensure fairness. Bunched orders must have the account designation before being executed. The daily allocating of contracts to various accounts is done and confirmed by the CTA, using preset instructions that treat all accounts equally. The FCM must also identify which accounts are included in bunched orders.

DELIVERY OF A COMMODITY

Any particular commodity is traded numerous times before it is actually delivered. There is a process that contracts go through before this happens. The delivery of a commodity can occur only within specific times indicated in a contract. The broker of the seller (the delivery occurs at the seller's convenience) gives a 'notice of intention to deliver' for the first day delivery is possible. The first possible delivery day is the 'first notice day'. This notice can be transferable. Unless otherwise arranged by the recipient, delivery of the commodity occurs the next business day following the day that the 'notice of intention to deliver' is given. Between the first notice day and actual delivery, the clearing house will have determined all of its long customers and will assign delivery to the oldest net long account.

Discretionary Account Regulation

SUBSECTION "SUPERVISION" OF SUPPLEMENTAL CHECKLIST FOR FCMS

The Supplemental Checklist for FCMs-Supervision requires Member firms to supervise all of their accounts and to have a written procedure for the supervision of discretionary accounts. Specifically, all discretionary accounts must be clearly identified, have regular, written reviews, and have power of attorney initiation and termination in writing. Only qualified persons are permitted to deal with discretionary accounts (i.e. APs with **less than** 2 years continuous experience as an active registrant are **not qualified**.) Accounts controlled by outside persons, must have the person's trading authorization in writing. Accounts of employees of other Member firms must have written trading authorization from a qualified contact person from the other firm. Regular communication of trades of such an account must be maintained. Any customer that buys deep 'out of the money" options must be given the required risk disclosure statement. All fees and charges must be explained in writing. The FCM must prohibit trading accounts of employees of exchanges and regulatory agencies. Commodity pool and omnibus accounts must be reviewed regularly to determine their financial status. Any pension fund accounts or investment company accounts must comply with "CFTC interpretation #10".

NFA'S RULE 2-8

NFA's rule 2-8 Discretionary Accounts essentially states that discretionary accounts require written authorization(Time and price decisions do not require written authorization). There must be a written power of attorney or other legally binding instrument that states the authorization to exercise discretion (i.e. make trading decisions on behalf of customer) over a customer's commodity futures, foreign futures, or foreign options account. Also, the Member must have records that clearly show which accounts they have discretionary authority over. Of course, the Member can only exercise discretion over those accounts. When a Member trades in a discretionary manner, it will be presumed that authorization to do so has already been obtained. (If individuals who own the account and have discretion over the account are from the same family, then they are exempt from the discretionary rules.) The Member must have a qualified person regularly review their discretionary trades to verify that these rules are being adhered to. The qualified person's review must be in writing.

TRADE IN FOREIGN FUTURES AND/OR OPTIONS

National Futures Association (NFA) Compliance Rule 2-8 requires all members to have written authorization from a customer in order to trade in a customer's discretionary account. Compliance Rule 2-8 states, in part, that an NFA member or associate cannot exercise discretion with regard to foreign futures or foreign options transactions on behalf of a customer unless the customer or account controller has specifically given written authorization for the member or associate to exercise such discretion. As with all transactions, written authorization should be provided in the form of a power of attorney or other such instrument.

ON-SITE VISITS OF BRANCH OFFICES OR GUARANTEED IBS

On-site inspections of branch offices or the offices of guaranteed IBs should include the review of discretionary accounts. Discretionary accounts require that the customer grants written permission in the form of power of attorney, to trade for the account. The proof of authorization to be discretionary should be reviewed. Orders for discretionary accounts should be clearly identified as discretionary. The procedures for supervising discretionary accounts should be reviewed, and the personnel responsible for supervising the accounts should be observed. If the office accepts block orders, it should be confirmed that non-discretionary orders are not included with discretionary orders. Split fills should be allocated according to the pre set program. Records of this should be reviewed and confirmed.

Promotional Material (Compliance Rule 2-29)

"PROMOTIONAL MATERIALS" PERTAINING TO COMMODITY FUTURES PRODUCTS

Though 'Promotional Materials' applies to communication with the public, it does not refer to routine daily contact with customers. It includes any written or verbal communication that concerns commodity futures accounts, agreements or transactions, which is directed at or distributed to the general public. It includes information intended to solicit futures accounts from the public. The content of these promotional materials is subject to specific content standards. The NFA must review and approve such content 10 days prior to its first use. Non-compliance can result in penalties. Mediums of distribution include printed materials such as newspapers; television or radio broadcast programming; and electronic distribution via the internet. Distribution also includes seminars and oral presentations intended for live, in-person audience and presentations given over the phone.

ELEMENTS NOT INCLUDED IN PROMOTIONAL MATERIAL

Promotional material for commodity futures products must <u>not</u> include:

- Fraudulent or deceptive information
- Claims that futures trading is good for everyone, anyone
- Unbalanced profit and loss claims (i.e. profit claims are prominent, loss risk warnings are obscure)including past performance statistics that are not countered with the statement that they do not indicative of future results
- Paid testimonials that omit the fact that they are paid
- Misstatements of facts or omission of a fact that makes the information misleading
- Past performance statistics of actual accounts unless the numbers are verifiable to the NFA to be representative of actual performance of reasonably comparable accounts during the same time period
- Information that is part of high pressure strategies

ELEMENTS USED BY BROKER-DEALERS SPECIFICALLY REFERRING TO SECURITY FUTURES PRODUCTS

The content of promotional materials that are used by broker-dealers that specifically refer to security futures products must include:

1. The Member's identity.
2. Contact information to access disclosure statements about the products.
3. A disclaimer that a futures position cannot be liquidated easily at any time and that futures are not best for all customers.
4. Origin date of the material.

90

5. Cumulative performance history, if any, of the trading programs experienced by the firm's customers. If there is no performance history, the material should say so.
6. Any conflict of interest of the firm with the security futures product.
7. Only legible text.
8. If it is intended for mass distribution, only content that has already been reviewed and approved by NFA 10 days prior to its first use. If the promotional language describing products is listed only in the member's services, then this requirement does not apply.

REQUIRED RECORD KEEPING

When an NFA Member uses promotional material, copies and /or transcripts of that material must be maintained and made available for examination by NFA. A record of the NFA review and approval that was required before the promotional material could be used must also be kept and made available. If the promotional material describes results, the Member must provide the basis for claiming those results to the NFA, if requested to do so. A Member may be required to file copies of all promotional material with the NFA promptly after the first time it is used.

GENERAL CHECKLIST SUBSECTION "PROMOTIONAL MATERIALS"

General Checklist –Promotional Material requires that Member firms have written procedures that govern the creation and use of promotional material. Before it can be used, promotional material must have the written approval of a qualified supervisor, other than the person(s) who created the material. Copies of promotional material and all documents that support the material used by the firm must be kept and maintained for 5 years. The material must contain balanced statements of profit vs. loss, past performance vs. future results, and opinion vs. fact. It must not be misleading. It must state that terms like "limited-risk" and "no margin call" pertain only to the purchase of options, that outside sources for ratings have limitations, and that hypothetical results pertain to programs that have only had 3 months or less of actual trading (NFA Compliance Rule 2-29(c)). Promotional content must not include certain claims such as ones about seasonal trades, historical price moves, or leverage as means to certain large profits.

DISCLAIMER STATEMENT REQUIRED FOR HYPOTHETICAL COMPOSITE PERFORMANCE STATEMENTS

Rule 2-29 regarding Hypothetical Performance results also describes the NFA Disclaimer for hypothetical composite performance record. These results attempt to show what multi-advisor or pool accounts could have obtained if "assets had been allocated among particular trading advisors" and the particular trading program used. The NFA Disclaimer for composite performance records is similar to hypothetical performance results for individual accounts. The main difference is that the composite performance disclaimer must state that the trading advisors have NOT traded together in the way described, the results were based on the "historical rate of return of the trading advisors", and because the allocation of assets changes the composite performance record could be distorted if it did not

Copyright © Mometrix Media. You have been licensed one copy of this document for personal use only. Any other reproduction or redistribution is strictly prohibited. All rights reserved.

account for these changes. Members with less than 1 year experience with allocating assets among trading advisors must state this fact to the customer. If a member is going to use hypothetical performance results, then all past performance results for comparable trades from the last five years must be included.

REQUIREMENTS FOR HYPOTHETICAL STATEMENTS

NFA rule 2-29 regarding Promotional material includes requirements relating to hypothetical statements. Hypothetical performance results are presented as results that could have been achieved if a certain trading program had been used. If this information is used, the NFA requires that the NFA disclaimer be included. This disclaimer is very specific and should be well known by all Members. The NFA Disclaimer on Hypothetical results essentially states that hypothetical performance results are just that, 'hypothetical'. It goes on to state that there are frequently sharp differences between hypothetical results and actual results obtained when using the same trading program. Hypothetical statements rely on hindsight, are not influenced by actual financial risk, and are not subject to the typical market pressures. It also states that if the Member or Associate has less than 1 year of actual trading experience, then this fact must be disclosed to the customer prior to trading. The customer should be advised to be cautious about relying on hypothetical performance results.

REQUIREMENTS FOR SFP PROMOTIONAL MATERIALS

Promotional material that is used to promote SFPs (Security Futures Products) to the general public must be reviewed and approved by the NFA ten days before its intended use. Other materials not intended for the general public can be submitted voluntarily. If the material has been created by third party advertising firms or consultants, then the material must still be submitted for review. It is still the responsibility of the Member firm to verify the accuracy and compliance of the promotional materials. If material is reprinted, then the firm reprinting it is responsible for verifying compliance with NFA rule 2-29 on promotional materials.

USE OF PAST OR PROJECTED PERFORMANCE

National Futures Association (NFA) Compliance Rule 2-29 stipulates that during the first three months for a new futures trading program, a firm may use hypothetical performance figures on their statements. However, these statements must clearly indicate that the projected performance is hypothetical in nature. After three months has passed, projected performance can no longer be hypothetical. Instead it must be based on a past rate of return earned in actual client separate accounts, incorporating Commodity Futures Trading Commission (CFTC) Regulations. The firm must state that it is projecting the performance on a going-forward basis using past results. There must be a clearly written statement laying out the fact that past performance is not an indication of future results. When projections of performance are based on actual client data, it must take into consideration all client accounts. Cherry-picking is not allowed. In addition, it is unethical to claim that there is an average rate of return when, in actuality, there was a wide swing or fluctuation in the rates of return earned by a firm's clients. The term *annual return* may not be used until the trading program has been in place for a period of 12 months. Any fees that a client can be expected to be responsible for paying must be represented in the rates of return referenced in any promotional material.

REPRINTS OF ARTICLES FROM INDUSTRY PUBLICATIONS

A firm may reprint articles from industry publications. However, doing so does not waive the firm from their responsibility to confirm the data and representations made in such publications. A firm cannot reprint an article and then claim it was not aware of the statements made within it or that it is not responsible or liable for any inaccurate claims held within it. In essence, reprinting an article carries the same weight as creating new promotional materials would.

PROHIBITED CONTENT

In general, NFA Rule 2-29 regarding communication with the public prohibits information which is fraudulent or deceitful, is part of a high pressure approach, and/or states that futures trading is appropriate for all persons. Promotional materials are prohibited from including content that:

- is likely to deceive the public
- contains any material misstatement of fact or purposely omits any fact, which renders the promotional material misleading
- mentions the possibility of profit without an equally prominent statement of the risk of loss
- makes reference to actual past trading profits without a disclaimer that such results are not necessarily indicative of future results
- includes any specific numerical or statistical information regarding the past financial performance and rate of return of any actual accounts, unless such information meets specific requirements and regulations set by the CFTC
- includes any testimonial that does not prominently feature displayed statements indicating that the testimonial is neither indicative of future performance nor provided in exchange for compensation, and that the testimonial is not representative of all reasonably comparable accounts

RULES INTENDED TO CODIFY THE CEA REQUIREMENTS TO GOVERN SALES PRACTICES

National Futures Association (NFA) Rule 2-29 regarding promotional materials is one of a number of such rules intended to codify the Commodity Exchange Act (CEA) requirement to "establish minimum standards governing the sales practices of its members" and other associated persons. It is intended to augment other related compliance rules. These other related rules are as follows:

- Rule 2-14 regulates the advertising of commodity pool operators (CPOs) and commodity trading advisors (CTAs).
- Rule 2-2 applies to all members and associated persons (AP). It is concerned with fraud and deceit, and essentially requires that high ethical standards related to customer relationships be met.

- Rule 2-4 also applies to all members and associated persons (AP). It is concerned with just and equitable principles of trade, and requires that high commercial honor standards be met.

Anti-Money Laundering Requirements

SUSPICIOUS ACTIVITY

Securities dealers are obligated to report activity that could be tied to money laundering. The industry has identified four red flags that point to suspicious activity that should be reported.

1. If the broker-dealer knows that money involved in the transaction is the result of criminal activity or that the transaction is intended to disguise illegal activity, the transaction must be reported.
2. If the broker-dealer would be required to engage in criminal activity in order to complete a requested transaction, it must be reported.
3. If the broker-dealer is aware that the purpose of the transaction is to circumvent the provisions of the Bank Secrecy Act, the transaction must be reported.
4. The last red flag requires the broker-dealer to consider the purpose that will be served by the transaction. If the broker-dealer cannot identify a legitimate purpose for a particular transaction based on available facts, the transaction should be reported as suspicious.

MINIMUM REQUIREMENTS TO ENSURE MEMBER COMPLIANCE

The following are four of the minimum program requirements intended to ensure member compliance with Commodity Futures Trading Commission (CFTC) regulations and the anti-money laundering regulations of the Bank Secrecy Act and the Department of the Treasury:

- the establishment and implementation of reasonably designed policies, procedures, and internal controls that are sufficient to ensure compliance with the applicable provisions of the Bank Secrecy Act and implementing regulations
- the establishment of an independent testing compliance program administered by a member or a similarly qualified outside party
- the designation and assignment of an individual or individuals who will assume responsibility for the implementation and monitoring of daily operations and internal program controls
- the establishment of a continuous training program for appropriate personnel

ANTI-MONEY LAUNDERING REGULATIONS

Money laundering is a term used to describe the process of moving funds derived from unlawful activity through the financial system until it appears that it has come from lawful sources. Futures accounts are especially vulnerable to being used in money laundering.

The International Money Laundering Abatement and Anti-Terrorist Financing Act requires, among other things, that all financial institutions establish anti-money laundering (AML) programs. These programs must include internal policies, procedures and controls that will deter, detect and report suspicious activity; a compliance officer to oversee the program; an employee training program; and a means of testing the effectiveness of the program.

Because trading accounts carried by FCMs and IBs are convenient laundering vehicles, the NFA has determined that member FCMs and IBs must comply with this Act, and implement AML programs. FCMs should also have customer identification procedures.

SUPPLEMENTAL CHECKLIST FOR FCMS SUBSECTION AML

The Supplemental Checklist for FCMs-AML (Anti-Money Laundering plan) requires Member firms to implement AML identification strategies that will prevent high risk accounts from being opened. The Member firm's compliance officer should have ready access to senior management and be free to report the findings. The identities of new customers must be confirmed. One of the ways this can be accomplished is by having a standardized customer identification program (CIP). The CIP should include checking the federal NCCT (uncooperative countries list), terrorist organization list, or the SDN report (Specially Designated Nationals and Blocked Persons) to see if the potential customer is included there. If the potential customer is from one of the listed countries, but are still found eligible to open an account, then the trading activity of the customer must be monitored regularly. If the potential customer is found to be included on the other lists, the FCM is required to notify the OFAC (Office of Foreign Assets Control) and follow their instructions on how to proceed.

SIGNS OF MONEY LAUNDERING

Anti –Money Laundering rules require that suspicious activities be reported. The kind of behavior that qualifies as suspicious behavior depends in part on the customer and their unique situation. This is why it is important for Members to know their customer very well. Some of this behavior has been summarized by FinCen. Here are some examples that could be signs of money laundering.

1. Behavior not consistent with a particular profession.
2. Repeated large personal deposits
3. Reluctance to identify oneself upon request
4. Wiring funds immediately after the funds clear.
5. Transfers of traveler's checks from countries on the 'non- cooperative' list compiled by FATF (Financial Action Task force on Money)
6. Having multiple bank accounts without logical reasons

AML OBLIGATIONS IMPOSED BY THE US PATRIOT ACT

The US Patriot Act was adopted following the September 11, 2001, terrorist attacks. According to the language in the summary of the act, the goal was to improve the government's ability to detect, prevent, and prosecute money-laundering activities.

Specifically, the US Patriot Act specifies that a financial institution's Anti-Money Laundering (AML) Program must be in writing and at a minimum must include the following:

1. Development of internal policies, procedures, and controls
2. The designation of a compliance officer
3. An official ongoing employee training program
4. An independent audit function to test the functionality of AML programs

Series 30 Practice Test

1. Are statements of opinion allowed to be used in promotional material?

   a. Yes, as long as they are identified as opinions

   b. Yes, as long as the statements are clearly identified as opinions and have a reasonable basis in fact

   c. Yes, statements of opinion are always allowed.

   d. No, statements of opinion are never allowed.

2. For how long must promotional material be kept on file from the date of its last use?

   a. 3 years

   b. 6 years

   c. 10 years

   d. 5 years

3. Which of the following transactions would be reportable under the Bank Secrecy Act?

   a. $15,000 cash deposit

   b. $15,000 ACH deposit

   c. $15,000 check deposit

   d. $15,000 fed fund wire deposit

4. Which of the following is often referred to as the "Anti-Money Laundering" (AML) Law?

   a. USA PATRIOT Act

   b. Sarbanes Oxley Act

   c. Bank Secrecy Act

   d. Securities Act of 1933

5. How often must member firms of FINRA conduct AML training for their personnel?

   a. Semiannually

   b. Annually

   c. Quarterly

   d. Biannually

6. Which of the following is NOT a general standard of promotional material according to Rule 2-29?

   a. May not be deceptive or misleading

   b. May not use high-pressure sales tactics

   c. May not be part of a high-pressure approach

   d. May imply that futures or forex trading is appropriate for everyone

7. What is the process of highlighting the performance of isolated accounts or isolated trades within an account called?

    a. Day-to-Day Communications
    b. Extracted Performance
    c. Cherry Picking
    d. Churning

8. Which of the following are examples of a discussion of profit?

    I. Past performance results
    II. Graphs depicting the growth of an account
    III. Discussion of opportunity
    IV. Statements that imply or infer profit

    a. I and II only
    b. IV only
    c. I, II, and IV
    d. I, II, III, and IV

9. Which of the following items are not required to be obtained from individuals under the NFA Know Your Customer Rule?

    a. Date of birth
    b. Net Worth
    c. Annual Income
    d. Spouse's name

10. How often must the FCM member carrying the customer account contact an individual active customer to verify that information on record is correct and give that individual an opportunity to correct or complete it?

    a. At least semi-annually
    b. At least annually
    c. At least every 2 years
    d. At least every 3 years

11. How must a customer give discretionary trading authorization to a stated individual or individuals?

    a. By phone
    b. In writing
    c. By phone or in writing
    d. No authorization is needed

12. When may a member or registered representative exercise discretionary power in a customer's account?

 a. As soon as the customer provides written authorization to a stated individual or individuals

 b. After the customer provides written authorization to a stated individual or individuals and it is submitted to the member

 c. After the customer provides written authorization to a stated individual or individuals and the member has approved the account as evidenced in writing by the member

 d. Anytime

13. Which of the following is an example of discretionary trading by a registered representative (RR)?

 a. A customer calls and instructs the RR to enter a trade to buy 100 shares of ABC Corp. at the market

 b. A customer calls and instructs the RR to enter a trade to buy 100 shares of ABC Corp. at a limit of $95.50, good until cancelled

 c. A customer calls and instructs the RR to enter a trade to sell 100 shares of ABC Corp. at the market

 d. A registered representative enters a trade to buy 100 shares of ABC Corp. at the market without contacting the customer

14. When must a trade order be identified as a discretionary?

 a. At order entry

 b. By market close the day the order is entered

 c. Any time before the trade settlement date

 d. Never

15. How often must discretionary trading be reviewed?

 a. Rarely without a written record of the review

 b. Rarely with a written record of the review

 c. Frequently without a written record of the review

 d. Frequently with a written record of the review

16. When must information concerning the costs associated with futures contracts be made available to customers?

 a. Before the account is opened

 b. Prior to the commencement of trading

 c. No later than when placing the initial trade

 d. Prior to the initial trade settlement date

17. What are the minimum initial and maintenance margin levels for security futures set by the CFTC and SEC?

a. 30% (initial) and 25% (maintenance) of the current market value of the positions

b. 25% (initial) and 25% (maintenance) of the current market value of the positions

c. 25% (initial) and 25% (maintenance) of the current market value of the positions

d. 20% (initial) and 20% (maintenance) of the current market value of the positions

18. Many futures and options contracts are limited on the number of contracts that may be held or controlled by one person. These limits are set by:

a. SEC & CFTC Regulations

b. CFTC Regulations

c. CFTC Regulations & the exchange where the contracts are traded

d. The exchange where the contracts are traded

19. Block trading is prohibited in which of the following accounts?

a. Proprietary accounts

b. Accounts in which your firm or an associated person employed by the firm has an interest or discretionary authority

c. Accounts for customers with whom your firm or an associated person has shared material non-public information

d. All of the above

20. Which of the following is true regarding the risk disclosure statement?

a. It must be provided to a customer before the time the account is approved to trade security futures

b. It must be provided to a customer at or before the time the account is approved to trade security futures.

c. The customer must sign an acknowledgement or receipt

d. You do not need to document that you provided the risk disclosure statement to the customer.

21. What is a stop loss order?

a. An order to sell a security at the current market price to avoid any additional losses

b. An order to sell a security at a specific price to avoid a potential loss

c. An order to sell a security that becomes a market order when the market trades at a specific price.

d. An order to sell a security that becomes a limit order when the market trades at a specific price.

22. For which of the following can security futures contacts not be used?

a. Speculation
b. Risk Management
c. Hedging
d. Capital Growth

23. Which of the following is false regarding the issuance of margin calls?

a. FCMs are required to make a bona fide attempt to collect required margin.
b. Required margin calls will be made within 1 business day after the even triggering the call.
c. FCMs are required to keep written records of all margin calls.
d. Firms must collect for margin on day trades.

24. How often must accounts be reviewed to determine margin calls?

a. Hourly
b. Twice per day
c. Daily
d. Weekly

25. Which of the following are reasons that upfront fees and expenses must be disclosed in the Disclosure Document?

a. Upfront fees and expenses affect net performance.
b. Investors should be fully aware of the amount of the upfront fees and expenses.
c. None of the above
d. Both A and B

26. What is the effect of upfront fees and organizational expenses on net performance?

a. Upfront fees and expenses increase net performance.
b. Upfront fees and expenses decrease net performance.
c. Upfront fees and expenses have no effect on net performance.
d. Upfront fees and expenses may either increase or decrease net performance.

27. Which of the following may accept funds from customers?

a. Introducing Broker (IB)
b. Futures Commission Merchant (FCM)
c. Both IB and FCM
d. None of the above

28. In general, what is the minimum net capital requirement for a Futures Commission Merchant (FCM)?

a. $500,000
b. $1,000,000
c. $1,500,000
d. $2,000,000

29. Which of the following are true regarding Guarantee Agreements?

> I. It must include the name of the FCM.
> II. It must include the name of the IB.
> III. It must include the effective date.
> IV. It must be signed and dated by an appropriate person from both the FCM and IB.
> V. In order to terminate the agreement, both parties must give written notice.

   a. I and II
   b. I, II, III, IV
   c. II, III, IV
   d. I, II, III, IV, V

30. What is the proficiency requirement for an individual applying for NFA membership as a CPO or CTA unless they are eligible for an alternative?

   a. Series 3
   b. Series 7
   c. Series 31
   d. Series 32

31. In regards to bunched orders, which of the following is NOT a responsibility of the futures commission merchant (FCM)?

   a. Maintain records that, as applicable, identify each order subject to post-execution allocation and the accounts to which the contracts were allocated
   b. Must receive sufficient information from an account manager to allow it to perform its functions
   c. Allocate contracts executed through a bunched order
   d. If there is notice of unusual allocation activity, must make a reasonable inquiry into the matter and, if appropriate, refer the matter to the proper regulatory authorities (e.g., the CFTC or NFA or its DSRO).

32. What are the 2 kinds of journals that must be establish and maintained for each commodity pool?

   a. Cash Receipts and Disbursement Journal & General Ledge
   b. Cash Receipts and Disbursement Journal & General Journal
   c. General Journal & Redemptions Payable
   d. General Ledger & Gain (Loss) on Investment in Commodity Pool

33. Which of the following is not a required Financial Statement that CPOs are required to file?

   a. Balance Sheet
   b. Statement of Changes in Net Asset Value
   c. Cash Flow Statement
   d. Income Statement

34. If a commodity pool has net assets of more than $500,000 at the start of its fiscal year, how often must it prepare its financial statements?

    a. Monthly
    b. Bimonthly
    c. Quarterly
    d. Annually

35. What information must be on the cover page of the Statement of Additional Information?

    I. The name of the commodity pool
    II. The date of the Statement of Additional Information
    III. A table of contents
    IV. The date of the most recent Disclosure document for the pool

    a. I and II
    b. I, II, and III
    c. I, II, and IV
    d. I, II, III, and IV

36. When must a CPO deliver (or cause to be delivered) a Statement of Additional Information to a prospective participant before accepting and receiving funds from him/her?

    a. A Statement of Additional Information is always required
    b. When required to register its securities under the Securities Act of 1933
    c. When required to register its securities under the Securities Act of 1934
    d. A Statement of Additional Information is never required. It is always optional.

37. How long can a CTA/CPO use a Disclosure Document as long as there are no material changes to be made?

    a. 6 months
    b. 12 months
    c. 18 months
    d. 24 months

38. Which organization is responsible for reviewing all Disclosure Documents?

    a. FINRA
    b. NFA
    c. SEC
    d. MSRB

39. Which of the following is false regarding a Disclosure Document for a CPO?

    a. It should be written in plain English.
    b. It should normally be 30 pages or less in length.
    c. The use of glossaries is not allowed.
    d. The cover page must include the Risk Disclosure Statement.

40. How long must the required books and records be kept?

    a. 3 years
    b. 4 years
    c. 5 years
    d. 6 years

41. Which of the following books and records must be stored in hard copy form rather than micro-graphic of electronic storage media?

    a. Financial Statements
    b. Customer Statements
    c. Customer Order Tickets
    d. General Ledger

42. When must the FCM time-stamp a customer order?

    a. When the order is received
    b. When the order is placed
    c. When the order is executed
    d. All of the above

43. Which of the following items should be addressed in a business continuity and disaster recovery plan?

    a. Back-up facilities, systems, and personnel
    b. Back-up copies of essential documents and data
    c. Communication plan
    d. All of the above

44. Within how many days must a sponsor notify NFA after the termination of an Associated Person?

    a. 1 Day
    b. 2 Days
    c. 15 Days
    d. 30 Days

45. An arbitration claim or notice of intent to arbitrate must be received by NFA within what period of time from the date the party filing the claim knew or should have known of the act or transaction that is the subject of the claim?

    a. 6 months
    b. 1 year
    c. 2 years
    d. There is no period of time. A claim may always be filed.

46. Which two reports are CPOs required to distribute to pool participants?

    a. Statement of Additional Information (SAI) and Annual Report
    b. Semi-Annual Report and Annual Report
    c. Account Statement and Semi-Annual Report
    d. Account Statement and Annual Report

47. Which of the following is true regarding annual reports?

a. It must contain information for the preceding fiscal year.
b. It must be distributed to pool participants within 60 days after the end of the fiscal year.
c. It must be filed with NFA.
d. It does not need to be certified by an independent certified public accountant.

48. How often must on-site inspections take place to satisfy NFA's supervisory requirement?

a. Annually
b. Every 2 years
c. Every 3 years
d. Every 6 years

49. Which of the following topics should be addressed in ethics training?

a. How to act honestly and fairly in the best interests of customers
b. Obtaining and assessing customers' financial situation and investment experience
c. How to establish effective supervisory systems and internal controls
d. All of the above

50. Supervising day-to-day activities includes which of the following areas?

I. Hiring
II. Registration
III. Customer information
IV. Account activity in customer accounts
V. Account activity in AP personal accounts

a. I & II only
b. I, II, & III
c. I, II, III, IV
d. I, II, III, IV, V

Answer Key and Explanations

1. B: Statements of opinion are allowed to be used in promotional material as long as the statements are clearly identified as opinions and have a reasonable basis in fact.

2. D: Promotional material must be kept on file for 5 years from the date of its last use. During the first 2 years of the 5 year period, the file must be in a readily accessible location.

3. A: Only cash deposits totaling $10,000 or more in a single day are reportable under the Bank Secrecy Act. Deposits of funds by ACH, check, and fed fund wire are not reportable.

4. C: The Bank Secrecy Act is often referred to as the "Anti-Money Laundering" (AML) Law.

5. B: Member firms must provide anti-money laundering training annually for their personnel.

6. D: Promotional material may NOT say or imply that futures or forex trading is appropriate for everyone. Promotional material may not be deceptive or misleading, may not use high-pressure sales tactics, and may not be part of a high-pressure approach. Therefore, answers A, B, and C are incorrect as they are general standards of promotional material according to Rule 2-29.

7. C: Cherry Picking is the process of highlighting the performance of isolated accounts or isolated trades within an account. A is incorrect because day-to-day communications are spontaneous communications that respond to a particular person's needs and concerns. B is incorrect because extracted performance is when a member highlights the performance of one component of a trading program. D is incorrect because churning is defined as excessive buying and selling in a customer's account mainly for the benefit of generating commissions for the broker.

8. D: All 4 items are examples of a discussion of profit.

9. D: The name of the individual's spouse is not required. However, the marital status and number of dependents of the individual are required items of information under the NFA Know Your Customer Rule. Date of birth, net worth, and annual income are also items that are required to be obtained under the NFA Know Your Customer Rule.

10. B: FCM members are required to contract an individual active customer at least annually. The customer may be contacted semi-annually, but it is not required so answer A is incorrect. Answers C and D are incorrect as those time periods are too long.

11. B: A customer must give a stated individual or individuals discretionary trading authorization in writing before any member or registered representative may exercise any discretionary power in the customer's account. Answers A and C are incorrect as a phone call is not an acceptable way to give discretionary trading authorization. Answer D is incorrect, because authorization is needed.

12. C: A member or registered representative may exercise discretionary power in a customer's account after the customer provides written authorization to a stated individual or individuals and the member has approved the account as evidenced in writing by the member. Answer A is incorrect as written authorization from the customer is only the first step of the approval process. Answer B is incorrect, because the member must approve the account before discretionary power may be exercised. Answer D is incorrect as the account must be approved by the member before discretionary power may be exercised.

13. D: When a registered representative enters a trade without receiving prior authorization from the customer, the RR has exercised discretionary power. Answers A, B, and C are incorrect, because a customer placing a trade with a registered representative is not discretionary.

14. A: A trade must be indicated as discretionary at order entry. Answers B and C are incorrect since those times are after the order has been placed. Answer D is incorrect since orders must be marked as discretionary.

15. D: Discretionary trading must be reviewed frequently and a written record of the review must be made. Answers A and B are incorrect, because discretionary trading must be reviewed frequently rather than rarely. Answer C is incorrect, because a written record of the review must be made.

16. B: Information concerning the costs associated with futures contracts must be made available to customers prior to the commencement of trading. Answer A is incorrect, because the information concerning costs does not need to be made prior to the account being opened. Answer C and D are incorrect, because the information on costs must be made before any trading is done.

17. D: The CFTC and the SEC have set minimum initial and maintenance margin levels for security futures at 20% of the current market value of the positions.

18. C: Part 150 of CFTC Regulations as well as the exchange where the contracts are traded set limits on the number of futures and options contracts that may be held or controlled by one person.

19. D: Block trading is prohibited in all the accounts listed.

20. B: The risk disclosure statement must be provided to a customer at or before the time the account is approved to trade security futures. A signed receipt is not required. However, you must document that the statement was provided to the customer.

21. C: A stop loss order is an order that becomes a market order when the market trades at a specific price. It is also called a stop order. Answer A is incorrect as it is a market order. Answers B and D are incorrect as selling at a specific price or better is a limit order.

22. D: Security futures contracts can be used for speculation, risk management, and hedging. They cannot be used for capital growth or income.

23. D: Firms are not required to collect or call for margin on day trades. Answers A, B, and C are true regarding the issuance of margin calls.

24. C: Accounts must be reviewed daily at the close of trading day to determine margin calls.

25. D: Upfront fees and expenses must be disclosed in the Disclosure Document, because investors should be fully aware of the amount of the fees and expenses as well as how they affect net performance.

26. B: Upfront fees and expenses decrease net performance.

27. B: Only a Futures Commission Merchant (FCM) may accept funds from customers as well as orders. Answer A is incorrect as an Introducing Broker (IB) may accept orders, but may not accept funds from customers.

28. B: In general, the minimum net capital amount is $1,000,000.

29. B: A Guarantee Agreement must include the names of the FCM and the IB, and have an effective date. Answer D is incorrect, because only 1 party must give written notice to terminate the agreement.

30. A: The Series 3, National Commodity Futures Examination, must be passed within 2 years prior to the individual's application to be registered as a CPO or CTA. Answers B, C, and D are incorrect, because the Series 7, Series 31, and Series 32 examinations are alternatives that an individual may be eligible for.

31. C: Allocating contracts executed through a bunched order is the responsibility of the CTA. Answers A, B, and D are incorrect as they are all responsibilities of the FCM.

32. B: The 2 kinds of journals that must be established and maintained for each commodity pool are a Cash Receipts and Disbursements Journal and a General Journal. The General Ledger consists of a group of individual accounts that include the Redemptions Payable and the Gain (Loss) on Investment in Commodity Pool.

33. C: CPOs are not required to file a Cash Flow Statement. They are required to file A Statement of Financial condition (Balance Sheet), an Income Statement, and a Statement of Changes in Net Asset Value.

34. A: A commodity pool that has more than $500,000 in net assets at the start of its fiscal year must prepare its financial statements monthly. If the net assets of the commodity pool are $500,000 or less, the financial statements must be prepared at least quarterly.

35. C: The cover page of the Statement of Additional Information must include the name of the commodity pool, the date of the most recent Disclosure Document for the pool, and the date of the Statement of Additional Information. It must also include a brief statement that the Statement of Additional Information is the second part of a two-part document and that it should be read in conjunction with the pool's Disclosure Document. The table of contents must be on the next page of the Statement of Additional Information.

36. B: A must CPO deliver (or cause to be delivered) a Statement of Additional Information to a prospective participant before accepting and receiving funds from the prospective participant when required to register its securities under the Securities Act of 1933.

37. B: A CTA/CPO may use a Disclosure Document for 12 months after it has been approved as long as it does not need to be updated sooner due to material changes to the information. The Disclosure Document must be reapproved after 12 months in order for its use to be continued.

38. B: The National Futures Association (NFA) is responsible for reviewing all Disclosure Documents. The CPO/CTA must submit the Document to the NFA and receive an acceptance letter from the NFA confirming that the Document can be used to solicit. Answers A, C, and D are incorrect since FINRA, the SEC, and the MSRB do not review Disclosure Statements.

39. C: The use of glossaries to define technical terms that cannot be avoided is encouraged. Answers A, B, and D are incorrect as they are true statements regarding Disclosure Documents for a CPO.

40. C: Books and records must be kept for 5 years and be in a readily accessible location for the first 2 years.

41. C: Customer order tickets (as well as trading cards) must be stored in hard copy form. Financial statements, customer statements, the general ledger, and most other books and records may be kept on micro-graphic or electronic storage media.

42. A: The FCM must time-stamp the order when it is received. Only option orders must also be time stamped when transmitted for execution.

43. D: Back-up facilities, systems, personnel, and copies of essential documents and data along with a communication plan are all items that should be addressed in a business continuity and disaster recovery plan.

44. D: NFA must be notified within 30 days of the termination of associated person from a sponsor.

45. C: An arbitration claim or notice of intent to arbitrate must be received by NFA within 2 years from the date when the party filing the Arbitration Claim knew or should have known of the act or transaction that is the subject of the claim.

46. D: CPOs are required to distribute an account statement and an annual report to pool participants. Statements of additional information and semi-annual reports are not required.

47. C: The annual report must be filed with NFA. Answers A, B, and D are incorrect as an annual report must contain information for two preceding fiscal years, be distributed to pool participants with 90 days after the end of the fiscal year and must be certified by an independent certified public accountant.

48. A: On-site inspections must be made annually in order to satisfy NFA's supervisory requirement.

49. D: Ethics training should include all of the topics listed.

50. D: Supervising day-to-day activities includes hiring, registration, customer information, and account activity of customer and AP personal accounts.

How to Overcome Test Anxiety

Just the thought of taking a test is enough to make most people a little nervous. A test is an important event that can have a long-term impact on your future, so it's important to take it seriously and it's natural to feel anxious about performing well. But just because anxiety is normal, that doesn't mean that it's helpful in test taking, or that you should simply accept it as part of your life. Anxiety can have a variety of effects. These effects can be mild, like making you feel slightly nervous, or severe, like blocking your ability to focus or remember even a simple detail.

If you experience test anxiety—whether severe or mild—it's important to know how to beat it. To discover this, first you need to understand what causes test anxiety.

Causes of Test Anxiety

While we often think of anxiety as an uncontrollable emotional state, it can actually be caused by simple, practical things. One of the most common causes of test anxiety is that a person does not feel adequately prepared for their test. This feeling can be the result of many different issues such as poor study habits or lack of organization, but the most common culprit is time management. Starting to study too late, failing to organize your study time to cover all of the material, or being distracted while you study will mean that you're not well prepared for the test. This may lead to cramming the night before, which will cause you to be physically and mentally exhausted for the test. Poor time management also contributes to feelings of stress, fear, and hopelessness as you realize you are not well prepared but don't know what to do about it.

Other times, test anxiety is not related to your preparation for the test but comes from unresolved fear. This may be a past failure on a test, or poor performance on tests in general. It may come from comparing yourself to others who seem to be performing better or from the stress of living up to expectations. Anxiety may be driven by fears of the future—how failure on this test would affect your educational and career goals. These fears are often completely irrational, but they can still negatively impact your test performance.

> **Review Video: <u>3 Reasons You Have Test Anxiety</u>**
> Visit mometrix.com/academy and enter code: 428468

Elements of Test Anxiety

As mentioned earlier, test anxiety is considered to be an emotional state, but it has physical and mental components as well. Sometimes you may not even realize that you are suffering from test anxiety until you notice the physical symptoms. These can include trembling hands, rapid heartbeat, sweating, nausea, and tense muscles. Extreme anxiety may lead to fainting or vomiting. Obviously, any of these symptoms can have a negative impact on testing. It is important to recognize them as soon as they begin to occur so that you can address the problem before it damages your performance.

> **Review Video: 3 Ways to Tell You Have Test Anxiety**
> Visit mometrix.com/academy and enter code: 927847

The mental components of test anxiety include trouble focusing and inability to remember learned information. During a test, your mind is on high alert, which can help you recall information and stay focused for an extended period of time. However, anxiety interferes with your mind's natural processes, causing you to blank out, even on the questions you know well. The strain of testing during anxiety makes it difficult to stay focused, especially on a test that may take several hours. Extreme anxiety can take a huge mental toll, making it difficult not only to recall test information but even to understand the test questions or pull your thoughts together.

> **Review Video: How Test Anxiety Affects Memory**
> Visit mometrix.com/academy and enter code: 609003

Effects of Test Anxiety

Test anxiety is like a disease—if left untreated, it will get progressively worse. Anxiety leads to poor performance, and this reinforces the feelings of fear and failure, which in turn lead to poor performances on subsequent tests. It can grow from a mild nervousness to a crippling condition. If allowed to progress, test anxiety can have a big impact on your schooling, and consequently on your future.

Test anxiety can spread to other parts of your life. Anxiety on tests can become anxiety in any stressful situation, and blanking on a test can turn into panicking in a job situation. But fortunately, you don't have to let anxiety rule your testing and determine your grades. There are a number of relatively simple steps you can take to move past anxiety and function normally on a test and in the rest of life.

> **Review Video: How Test Anxiety Impacts Your Grades**
> Visit mometrix.com/academy and enter code: 939819

Physical Steps for Beating Test Anxiety

While test anxiety is a serious problem, the good news is that it can be overcome. It doesn't have to control your ability to think and remember information. While it may take time, you can begin taking steps today to beat anxiety.

Just as your first hint that you may be struggling with anxiety comes from the physical symptoms, the first step to treating it is also physical. Rest is crucial for having a clear, strong mind. If you are tired, it is much easier to give in to anxiety. But if you establish good sleep habits, your body and mind will be ready to perform optimally, without the strain of exhaustion. Additionally, sleeping well helps you to retain information better, so you're more likely to recall the answers when you see the test questions.

Getting good sleep means more than going to bed on time. It's important to allow your brain time to relax. Take study breaks from time to time so it doesn't get overworked, and don't study right before bed. Take time to rest your mind before trying to rest your body, or you may find it difficult to fall asleep.

> **Review Video: <u>The Importance of Sleep for Your Brain</u>**
> Visit mometrix.com/academy and enter code: 319338

Along with sleep, other aspects of physical health are important in preparing for a test. Good nutrition is vital for good brain function. Sugary foods and drinks may give a burst of energy but this burst is followed by a crash, both physically and emotionally. Instead, fuel your body with protein and vitamin-rich foods.

Also, drink plenty of water. Dehydration can lead to headaches and exhaustion, especially if your brain is already under stress from the rigors of the test. Particularly if your test is a long one, drink water during the breaks. And if possible, take an energy-boosting snack to eat between sections.

> **Review Video: <u>How Diet Can Affect your Mood</u>**
> Visit mometrix.com/academy and enter code: 624317

Along with sleep and diet, a third important part of physical health is exercise. Maintaining a steady workout schedule is helpful, but even taking 5-minute study breaks to walk can help get your blood pumping faster and clear your head. Exercise also releases endorphins, which contribute to a positive feeling and can help combat test anxiety.

When you nurture your physical health, you are also contributing to your mental health. If your body is healthy, your mind is much more likely to be healthy as well. So take time to rest, nourish your body with healthy food and water, and get moving as much as possible. Taking these physical steps will make you stronger and more able to take the mental steps necessary to overcome test anxiety.

Mental Steps for Beating Test Anxiety

Working on the mental side of test anxiety can be more challenging, but as with the physical side, there are clear steps you can take to overcome it. As mentioned earlier, test anxiety often stems from lack of preparation, so the obvious solution is to prepare for the test. Effective studying may be the most important weapon you have for beating test anxiety, but you can and should employ several other mental tools to combat fear.

First, boost your confidence by reminding yourself of past success—tests or projects that you aced. If you're putting as much effort into preparing for this test as you did for those, there's no reason you should expect to fail here. Work hard to prepare; then trust your preparation.

Second, surround yourself with encouraging people. It can be helpful to find a study group, but be sure that the people you're around will encourage a positive attitude. If you spend time with others who are anxious or cynical, this will only contribute to your own anxiety. Look for others who are motivated to study hard from a desire to succeed, not from a fear of failure.

Third, reward yourself. A test is physically and mentally tiring, even without anxiety, and it can be helpful to have something to look forward to. Plan an activity following the test, regardless of the outcome, such as going to a movie or getting ice cream.

When you are taking the test, if you find yourself beginning to feel anxious, remind yourself that you know the material. Visualize successfully completing the test. Then take a few deep, relaxing breaths and return to it. Work through the questions carefully but with confidence, knowing that you are capable of succeeding.

Developing a healthy mental approach to test taking will also aid in other areas of life. Test anxiety affects more than just the actual test—it can be damaging to your mental health and even contribute to depression. It's important to beat test anxiety before it becomes a problem for more than testing.

Study Strategy

Being prepared for the test is necessary to combat anxiety, but what does being prepared look like? You may study for hours on end and still not feel prepared. What you need is a strategy for test prep. The next few pages outline our recommended steps to help you plan out and conquer the challenge of preparation.

STEP 1: SCOPE OUT THE TEST

Learn everything you can about the format (multiple choice, essay, etc.) and what will be on the test. Gather any study materials, course outlines, or sample exams that may be available. Not only will this help you to prepare, but knowing what to expect can help to alleviate test anxiety.

STEP 2: MAP OUT THE MATERIAL

Look through the textbook or study guide and make note of how many chapters or sections it has. Then divide these over the time you have. For example, if a book has 15 chapters and you have five days to study, you need to cover three chapters each day. Even better, if you have the time, leave an extra day at the end for overall review after you have gone through the material in depth.

If time is limited, you may need to prioritize the material. Look through it and make note of which sections you think you already have a good grasp on, and which need review. While you are studying, skim quickly through the familiar sections and take more time on the challenging parts. Write out your plan so you don't get lost as you go. Having a written plan also helps you feel more in control of the study, so anxiety is less likely to arise from feeling overwhelmed at the amount to cover.

STEP 3: GATHER YOUR TOOLS

Decide what study method works best for you. Do you prefer to highlight in the book as you study and then go back over the highlighted portions? Or do you type out notes of the important information? Or is it helpful to make flashcards that you can carry with you? Assemble the pens, index cards, highlighters, post-it notes, and any other materials you may need so you won't be distracted by getting up to find things while you study.

If you're having a hard time retaining the information or organizing your notes, experiment with different methods. For example, try color-coding by subject with colored pens, highlighters, or post-it notes. If you learn better by hearing, try recording yourself reading your notes so you can listen while in the car, working out, or simply sitting at your desk. Ask a friend to quiz you from your flashcards, or try teaching someone the material to solidify it in your mind.

STEP 4: CREATE YOUR ENVIRONMENT

It's important to avoid distractions while you study. This includes both the obvious distractions like visitors and the subtle distractions like an uncomfortable chair (or a too-comfortable couch that makes you want to fall asleep). Set up the best study environment possible: good lighting and a comfortable work area. If background music helps you focus, you may want to turn it on, but otherwise keep the room quiet. If you are using a computer to take notes, be sure you don't have any other windows open, especially applications like social media, games, or anything else that could distract you. Silence your phone and turn off notifications. Be sure to keep water close by so you stay hydrated while you study (but avoid unhealthy drinks and snacks).

Also, take into account the best time of day to study. Are you freshest first thing in the morning? Try to set aside some time then to work through the material. Is your mind clearer in the afternoon or evening? Schedule your study session then. Another method is to study at the same time of day that you will take the test, so that your brain gets used to working on the material at that time and will be ready to focus at test time.

STEP 5: STUDY!

Once you have done all the study preparation, it's time to settle into the actual studying. Sit down, take a few moments to settle your mind so you can focus, and begin to follow your study plan. Don't give in to distractions or let yourself procrastinate. This is your time to prepare so you'll be ready to fearlessly approach the test. Make the most of the time and stay focused.

Of course, you don't want to burn out. If you study too long you may find that you're not retaining the information very well. Take regular study breaks. For example, taking five minutes out of every hour to walk briskly, breathing deeply and swinging your arms, can help your mind stay fresh.

As you get to the end of each chapter or section, it's a good idea to do a quick review. Remind yourself of what you learned and work on any difficult parts. When you feel that you've mastered the material, move on to the next part. At the end of your study session, briefly skim through your notes again.

But while review is helpful, cramming last minute is NOT. If at all possible, work ahead so that you won't need to fit all your study into the last day. Cramming overloads your brain with more information than it can process and retain, and your tired mind may struggle to recall even previously learned information when it is overwhelmed with last-minute study. Also, the urgent nature of cramming and the stress placed on your brain contribute to anxiety. You'll be more likely to go to the test feeling unprepared and having trouble thinking clearly.

So don't cram, and don't stay up late before the test, even just to review your notes at a leisurely pace. Your brain needs rest more than it needs to go over the information again. In fact, plan to finish your studies by noon or early afternoon the day before the test. Give your brain the rest of the day to relax or focus on other things, and get a good night's sleep. Then you will be fresh for the test and better able to recall what you've studied.

STEP 6: TAKE A PRACTICE TEST

Many courses offer sample tests, either online or in the study materials. This is an excellent resource to check whether you have mastered the material, as well as to prepare for the test format and environment.

Check the test format ahead of time: the number of questions, the type (multiple choice, free response, etc.), and the time limit. Then create a plan for working through them. For example, if you have 30 minutes to take a 60-question test, your limit is 30 seconds per question. Spend less time on the questions you know well so that you can take more time on the difficult ones.

If you have time to take several practice tests, take the first one open book, with no time limit. Work through the questions at your own pace and make sure you fully understand them. Gradually work up to taking a test under test conditions: sit at a desk with all study materials put away and set a timer. Pace yourself to make sure you finish the test with time to spare and go back to check your answers if you have time.

After each test, check your answers. On the questions you missed, be sure you understand why you missed them. Did you misread the question (tests can use tricky wording)? Did you forget the information? Or was it something you hadn't learned? Go back and study any shaky areas that the practice tests reveal.

Taking these tests not only helps with your grade, but also aids in combating test anxiety. If you're already used to the test conditions, you're less likely to worry about it, and working through tests until you're scoring well gives you a confidence boost. Go through the practice tests until you feel comfortable, and then you can go into the test knowing that you're ready for it.

Test Tips

On test day, you should be confident, knowing that you've prepared well and are ready to answer the questions. But aside from preparation, there are several test day strategies you can employ to maximize your performance.

First, as stated before, get a good night's sleep the night before the test (and for several nights before that, if possible). Go into the test with a fresh, alert mind rather than staying up late to study.

Try not to change too much about your normal routine on the day of the test. It's important to eat a nutritious breakfast, but if you normally don't eat breakfast at all, consider eating just a protein bar. If you're a coffee drinker, go ahead and have your normal coffee. Just make sure you time it so that the caffeine doesn't wear off right in the middle of your test. Avoid sugary beverages, and drink enough water to stay hydrated but not so much that you need a restroom break 10 minutes into the test. If your test isn't first thing in the morning, consider going for a walk or doing a light workout before the test to get your blood flowing.

Allow yourself enough time to get ready, and leave for the test with plenty of time to spare so you won't have the anxiety of scrambling to arrive in time. Another reason to be early is to select a good seat. It's helpful to sit away from doors and windows, which can be distracting. Find a good seat, get out your supplies, and settle your mind before the test begins.

When the test begins, start by going over the instructions carefully, even if you already know what to expect. Make sure you avoid any careless mistakes by following the directions.

Then begin working through the questions, pacing yourself as you've practiced. If you're not sure on an answer, don't spend too much time on it, and don't let it shake your confidence. Either skip it and come back later, or eliminate as many wrong answers as possible and guess among the remaining ones. Don't dwell on these questions as you continue—put them out of your mind and focus on what lies ahead.

Be sure to read all of the answer choices, even if you're sure the first one is the right answer. Sometimes you'll find a better one if you keep reading. But don't second-guess yourself if you do immediately know the answer. Your gut instinct is usually right. Don't let test anxiety rob you of the information you know.

If you have time at the end of the test (and if the test format allows), go back and review your answers. Be cautious about changing any, since your first instinct tends to be correct, but make sure you didn't misread any of the questions or accidentally mark the wrong answer choice. Look over any you skipped and make an educated guess.

At the end, leave the test feeling confident. You've done your best, so don't waste time worrying about your performance or wishing you could change anything. Instead, celebrate the successful completion of this test. And finally, use this test to learn how to deal with anxiety even better next time.

> **Review Video: 5 Tips to Beat Test Anxiety**
> Visit mometrix.com/academy and enter code: 570656

Important Qualification

Not all anxiety is created equal. If your test anxiety is causing major issues in your life beyond the classroom or testing center, or if you are experiencing troubling physical symptoms related to your anxiety, it may be a sign of a serious physiological or psychological condition. If this sounds like your situation, we strongly encourage you to seek professional help.

Thank You

We at Mometrix would like to extend our heartfelt thanks to you, our friend and patron, for allowing us to play a part in your journey. It is a privilege to serve people from all walks of life who are unified in their commitment to building the best future they can for themselves.

The preparation you devote to these important testing milestones may be the most valuable educational opportunity you have for making a real difference in your life. We encourage you to put your heart into it—that feeling of succeeding, overcoming, and yes, conquering will be well worth the hours you've invested.

We want to hear your story, your struggles and your successes, and if you see any opportunities for us to improve our materials so we can help others even more effectively in the future, please share that with us as well. **The team at Mometrix would be absolutely thrilled to hear from you!** So please, send us an email (support@mometrix.com) and let's stay in touch.

> **If you'd like some additional help, check out these other resources we offer for your exam:**
> **http://MometrixFlashcards.com/Series30**

Additional Bonus Material

Due to our efforts to try to keep this book to a manageable length, we've created a link that will give you access to all of your additional bonus material.

> **Please visit**
> **https://www.mometrix.com/bonus948/series30 to**
> **access the information.**